The Quality Rubric

Also available from ASQ Quality Press:

There is Another Way!: Launch a Baldrige-Based Quality Classroom
Margaret A. Byrnes with Jeanne C. Baxter

Improving Student Learning: Applying Deming's Quality Principles in the Classroom, 2nd Edition
Lee Jenkins

Quality Across the Curriculum: Integrating Quality Tools and PDSA with Standards
Jay Marino and Ann Haggerty Raines

Permission to Forget: And Nine Other Root Causes of America's Frustration with Education
Lee Jenkins

Smart Teaching: Using Brain Research and Data to Continuously Improve Learning
Ronald J. Fitzgerald

Boot Camp for Leaders in K–12 Education: Continuous Improvement
Lee Jenkins, Lloyd O. Roettger, and Caroline Roettger

Thinking Tools for Kids: An Activity Book for Classroom Learning
Barbara A. Cleary and Sally J. Duncan

The Principal's Leadership Counts!: Launch a Baldrige-Based Quality School
Margaret A. Byrnes with Jeanne C. Baxter

Insights to Performance Excellence 2006: An Inside Look at the 2006 Baldrige Award Criteria
Mark L. Blazey

Successful Applications of Quality Systems in K–12 Schools
ASQ Quality Education Division

ASQ Z1.11-2002 Quality assurance standards: Guidelines for the application of ANSI/ISO/ASQ Q9001-2000 to education and training institutions
ASQ

To request a complimentary catalog of ASQ Quality Press publications,
call 800-248-1946, or visit our Web site at http://qualitypress.asq.org.

The Quality Rubric

A Systematic Approach for Implementing Quality
Principles and Tools in Classrooms and Schools

Steve Benjamin

ASQ Quality Press
Milwaukee, Wisconsin

American Society for Quality, Quality Press, Milwaukee 53203
© 2007 American Society for Quality
All rights reserved. Published 2006
Printed in the United States of America

12 11 10 09 08 07 06   5 4 3 2 1

Library of Congress Cataloging-in-Publication Data
Benjamin, Steve, 1950–
    The quality rubric : a systematic approach for implementing quality principles and tools in classrooms and
schools / Steve Benjamin.
        p. cm.
    Includes bibliographical references and index.
    ISBN 0-87389-703-X (pbk. : alk. paper)
    1. School improvement programs.   2. Values—Study and teaching.   3. School management and
organization.   I. Title.

    LB2822.8.B46 2007
    371.2—dc22   2006023494
    ISBN-10: 0-87389-703-X
    ISBN-13: 978-0-87389-703-7

Publisher: William A. Tony
Acquisitions Editor: Matt Meinholz
Project Editor: Paul O'Mara
Production Administrator: Randall Benson

ASQ Mission: The American Society for Quality advances individual, organizational, and community excellence
worldwide through learning, quality improvement, and knowledge exchange.

Attention Bookstores, Wholesalers, Schools, and Corporations: ASQ Quality Press books, videotapes, audio-
tapes, and software are available at quantity discounts with bulk purchases for business, educational, or instructional use. For information, please contact ASQ Quality Press at 800-248-1946, or write to ASQ Quality Press,
P.O. Box 3005, Milwaukee, WI 53201-3005.

To place orders or to request a free copy of the ASQ Quality Press Publications Catalog, including ASQ mem-
bership information, call 800-248-1946. Visit our Web site at www.asq.org or http://qualitypress.asq.org.

♾ Printed on acid-free paper

Quality Press
600 N. Plankinton Avenue
Milwaukee, Wisconsin 53203
Call toll free 800-248-1946
Fax 414-272-1734
www.asq.org
http://qualitypress.asq.org
http://standardsgroup.asq.org
E-mail: authors@asq.org

Contents

Figures and Tables

Foreword

I've been a superintendent for many years. I've always tried to bring quality to my work and to the organizations that I have led. But my district's formal "quality" journey began four or five years ago. As part of our growth and development, we've engaged in many quality initiatives and have even created our district improvement plan using the Baldrige framework as a guide. I know, however, that real growth in student learning will happen only when the interactions among teachers and students fundamentally change. Quality has to take root at the classroom level. When that happens, schools will become better and, in turn, our classrooms will improve as evidenced by quality measures.

To that end, we've invested many resources in the past several years on quality training for our instructional staff. I have personally helped lead the training in order to demonstrate the importance of implementing the quality philosophy and tools in schools. At this point, all our teachers and administrators have been trained, and we are beginning to work with support staff. However, until recently, we did not have a complete system in place to ensure that the attitudes and actions that we desired would, in fact, be demonstrated in each classroom across our district. We had not set clear expectations, and we had not developed a measuring system that would allow everyone to know when "quality" had become systemically entrenched. In the Baldrige system, we had identified an excellent approach or strategy, but we hadn't gone the next step, which was to monitor implementation or deployment of the approach. The best idea, if not implemented, will fail to produce results.

When we first saw *The Quality Rubric*, lightbulbs were switched on. I knew that this was the missing piece—the structure that was needed to help us get beyond talk about implementation to demonstrable data that would indicate degree of deployment. This book lays out a series of developmentally challenging activities that represent increasing levels of quality deployment. Dr. Benjamin indicates that districts can adapt the recommended rubric to fit their own needs, and we have done exactly that, although we didn't stray too far from the basic ideas contained in *The Quality Rubric*. We've taken the ideas and adapted them, adjusting vocabulary when necessary. We have created our own quality rubric and added a glossary of definitions to help everyone know and understand our quality expectations. Our Board of School Trustees has approved the final rubric, and we are set to implement. Finally, everyone knows what we expect—what "quality in the classroom" should look like. Our teachers can begin slowly and move at a pace that fits their own developmental levels, with clear expectations for continual growth. I can regularly report to my board how many classrooms are operating at Quality Levels 1, 2, 3, and 4. Additionally, we are developing a school building quality rubric to assess our schools (much like the one found in the final section of this book) in order to add yet another dimension to our quality journey and to our understanding of what quality in our district truly looks and feels like.

The Quality Rubric is a great resource for schools and districts that are truly committed to ensuring quality in the classroom. If you are serious about your quality quest, the ideas in this book will help advance you toward the realization of your goal.

Dr. John McKinney, Superintendent
Danville Community School Corporation
Danville, Indiana

Preface

These are the worst of times; these are the best of times, especially if you are an educator. Teachers and administrators face unparalleled federal, state, and local pressures for accountability—most often defined as the percentage of students mastering the state test. Teachers eat, sleep, and breathe standards, feeling unable to stray far from their curriculum guides, which are becoming more restrictive and prescriptive. Today's student population presents unique challenges never-before experienced. Poverty rates have increased in many schools, and the percentage of students whose first language is not English is rising—a challenging educational landscape, to say the least. Our boats are sailing into a strong headwind, and any progress at all should be celebrated.

There is a brighter side of the balance sheet, however. Today, technology can help us identify best practices at the speed of a Google search. (Feeling lucky today?) Education research is friendlier and more accessible than ever before. We find ourselves working more collaboratively. Professional learning communities (DuFour and Eaker, 1998) have opened the door for self-critique, peer-support, and continual improvement of teaching and learning. Today's classroom models involve our students as active learners; they have become codesigners of instruction, coevaluators of the success of learning activities, and coinitiators of needed improvements. Teachers have migrated to the shared decision-making model, as have many principals and superintendents. The "great leader" theory has been replaced with one in which leadership is ubiquitous, observed at all levels of the system. Today's leaders must be more adept at asking the correct questions and less concerned with always being able to provide the right answers (Heifetz and Laurie, 1997). Cooperation in continuous improvement of learning is everyone's responsibility, and this tectonic shift is making education more exciting, enjoyable, and successful. Educators are learning from other professions and fields, including health care and the world of business and management. Technology is also helping us gather, store, sort, and use data—new capabilities in many schools and classrooms. Teachers are learning to use data to change instruction and learning outcomes.

On balance, there are many reasons to be happy, excited, and hopeful.

In conducting research for *The Quality Rubric,* I read Stevens and Levi's (2005) *Introduction to Rubrics.* I like the way they designed the opening section of their book, so I have patterned my preface after theirs. In a sense, I am starting with a simple illustration of benchmarking—finding wonderful examples of excellence and attempting to mimic others' approaches.

PURPOSE OF *THE QUALITY RUBRIC*

The Quality Rubric is designed to teach you about "quality in education" and to provide a comprehensive framework that can be used to guide the gradual deployment of quality values, principles, tools, and techniques throughout your learning system. You will learn specific actions that can be taken in each of four performance levels to help you and your colleagues implement a quality education system in your classrooms, schools, and district. *The Quality Rubric helps people and organizations set clear expectations for implementation of "quality" learning, establishes a rubric to guide development, and provides a measurement tool to help gauge progress through four stages of growth.* When good quality learning is combined with clear expectations, a method of tracking deployment, and appropriate recognition, real improvement can be expected. Improved organizational performance results can occur only after good approaches have been selected and fully implemented. Approach. Deployment. Results.

This book, then, is designed to:

- Teach some of the most powerful quality in education concepts and tools to relative newcomers to this exciting field
- Position the learning within an integrated systems framework that provides a logical "flow" to the work

- Provide a mechanism that encourages the establishment of high expectations for deployment of the learning
- Establish a measurement device that can be used to track gradual implementation of the principles, tools, and techniques in your classrooms and schools

I have become disenchanted with staff development that goes nowhere. *The Quality Rubric* was written to help you leverage your quality in education learning for the benefit of students and other customers of education organizations.

INTENDED AUDIENCE

I have written this book for pre-K–12 educators, including teachers, administrators, and school board members. *The Quality Rubric* is intended for individuals who may know little or nothing about "quality in education," although I hope my words will be of interest to quality veterans, too, because many of you have most likely become discouraged at the slow rate at which your quality training is being implemented in classrooms and schools. You may be thinking, "We trained them; why aren't we seeing use of the ideas in classrooms?" This book is for you. Indirectly, my book is for students and parents, although I expect that teachers and principals will be the vehicle by which other target groups learn about the ideas found in *The Quality Rubric*. I hope that university faculty will find some of the concepts and tools useful, as there is often a mismatch between what students in teacher and administrator preparation programs learn and what they need to know to be successful in today's pre-K–12 educational environment.

I know that teachers, principals, and support staff are extremely busy. I want to respect their most valuable resource, time, so I have attempted to write in straightforward and uncomplicated prose. Each section is short and to the point, yet I believe I have given you enough information to make your way forward without too many U-turns.

Although I have provided some justification for my ideas by including quotations and references from experts in the quality improvement and related fields, I have limited the number of references purposefully. I hope you will be convinced of the correctness of the ideas in *The Quality Rubric* more because they make sense to you and less because a parade of experts tells you it's so. The most effective teachers I've known operate on instinct for what is best for their students, with sprinkles of expert advice added only when needed.

ACKNOWLEDGMENTS

I want to recognize the many wonderful teachers I've worked with over the past several years. They have taught me much about quality in the classroom and what is possible, even with our youngest students. I think of Diana and her proud kindergarten students who demonstrated that data folders and student-led conferences could lead to improved student results, increased student responsibility, and greater parent engagement and satisfaction. I remember Linda's team problem-solving activity, which resulted in a fishbone diagram of all the reasons why her students weren't making progress in meeting their reading goals. And Ardis and Beth, who took such interest and pride in improving their car-rider dismissal process, maintaining a mile-long run chart in the hallway to document their improvements. I also thank the many principals and superintendents who saw the benefit in bringing quality learning and systems into their schools.

There are many more colleagues who have helped me learn, and I thank you all.

Definitions

In order to provide you with an "advance organizer" (Ausubel, 1960) of some of the most important and frequently used terms and concepts in *The Quality Rubric,* I have included this short definitions section. You might want to scan these pages before launching into the book. When you encounter the terms later in the text, they should make more sense. If not, at least you know where to return for help. If you are already familiar with these quality terms, you may choose to proceed to Part 1.

alignment—When the various elements of the organization (classrooms within a school and schools within a district) have common purposes and goals and use agreed processes consistently. In an aligned system, everyone feels as if they are pulling in the same direction because goals are clear and linked, and everyone is expected to implement best-practice processes. Alignment is difficult to achieve without a clear understanding of the systems perspective.

benchmarking—The process of identifying organizations, known as benchmarks, that have much better processes and results than you do in order to implement similar approaches. School A learns that School B has managed, over several years, to generate much better reading performance. After discussions with, and visits to, School B, School A learns the secrets of School B's success and begins to implement those approaches.

continuous quality improvement—"Managing the continuous improvement of service delivery processes and outcomes through data-driven strategies and empowered staff to exceed customer expectations" (Smith, Discenza, and Piland, 1993, p. 35). CQI is also known by many other names, including total quality management (TQM). A related term, *quality in education,* signifies a branch of the quality field.

core value—A central belief that should guide a person's or an organization's talk and action. In our personal lives, we might value perseverance and honesty. In the world of continuous quality improvement, values such as teamwork, use of data to drive decision making, and systems thinking are common central beliefs. Core values can be used as filters to help us make appropriate decisions.

customer—Anyone who receives a product (ninth-grade teachers receiving students who have just completed the eighth grade) or service (students receiving extra tutoring help in order to master specific state academic standards). Education has internal customers (students are customers of teachers and other students; students are customers of support services such as the food services and transportation services departments) and external customers (local businesses that hire education's graduates; universities that accept students for further study). A related term is *stakeholder.*

customer and stakeholder matrix—A chart that lists the customers and stakeholders of some part of the system (district, school, or classroom) as well as their expressed needs and how those needs were identified. The stakeholder matrix information is used to ensure the proper organizational goal set. For example, if customers tell you that "very good math skills" is one of their expectations, the school can translate this need into clear goals and can engage in discussion about how to measure math performance for all students. Once measures have been set and baseline data are gathered, the school can identify needed improvements and key strategies. Customer needs, derived from the matrix, set the planning and improvement processes in motion.

dashboard—A set of performance indicators (for example, percentage of students reading on or above level, percentage attendance, number of office referrals for improper behavior) that reflect the most important results for the classroom, school, and district and that have been developed in participation with customers and stakeholders. The dashboard and the customer matrix should be aligned. The purpose of the dashboard is to help everyone focus on the most important goals, to provide data on current and desired performance, and to engender discussion about opportunities for improvement.

data folders—Three-ring binders, a series of Excel charts, or electronic lockers in which students, teachers, administrators, and support staff maintain their results data for dashboard performance indicators.

deployment—Implementation of key strategies, tactics, and action plans. Without systematic deployment of high-quality approaches, improved results will be elusive and fleeting. Quality organizations track degree of deployment to ensure full implementation of their most important approaches. *In essence, deployment is what The Quality Rubric is all about—taking your best knowledge, tools, and attitudes (quality education) and making sure these powerful approaches are fully implemented 24/7.*

flowchart—A graphic that shows a series of interrelated steps that, taken together, constitute a complete process. Documentation of a process. "A flowchart illustrates the step-by-step approach to a specific process by using a series of symbols to denote tasks, decision points, and stages in the flow of the process" (Cleary and Duncan, 1999, p. 160).

mission—The answer to the question, "Why do we come to work each day?" Similar to an organization's purpose. You can derive a concise mission by thinking about your customers' needs. Once you know what those needs are, you are well on your way to developing a clear sense of mission because essentially, an organization's mission is to meet or exceed its customers' expectations.

quality tools—Systematic methods and approaches designed to help educators, students, and support staff collect and analyze data, identify causes of problems, use data to identify best-practice strategies, and continually improve performance. Examples include fishbone analysis, affinity exercises, relationship diagrams, flowcharts, and Pareto diagrams, among many others.

plan-do-check-improve—The continuous improvement cycle, and although one can begin after any point in the process, most practitioners would start by setting a plan that includes clear goals and action steps along with timelines and personal responsibilities. The plan would then be implemented as specified, constituting the do step. Many organizations stop here, but in the quality world, careful attention is paid to checking the degree to which plans have been properly implemented and the interim performance results to determine how well the plan has worked. When results are unsatisfactory, the team improves by adjusting plans and tightening implementation. When results are satisfactory, the team "improves" by setting higher standards and adjusting plans accordingly. PDCI is also known as PDSA (plan-do-study-act) and PDCA (plan-do-check-act). All are also commonly referred to as the continuous improvement process.

rubric—A scoring tool that lays out specific performance expectations. Rubrics divide an assignment into its component parts and provide a detailed description of what constitutes acceptable or unacceptable levels of performance for each of those parts (Stevens and Levi, 2005). *In this book, specific "quality" activities have been assigned in each of four levels of performance; thus, a multilevel rubric has been provided to help guide continual improvement in your educational organization.*

S2S talks—Shorthand for System-to-System. There are numerous levels in a system. In education, we have the state department of education, the district or corporation, the school, the grade level, the classroom, and the student. S2S talks engage one level of the system with the next level in order to review strategy deployment and leading performance results, usually on a quarterly basis. The ultimate purpose is to review "progress to plan" and to make adjustments as needed.

student-led conferences—Parent-teacher-student meetings in which students use their data folders as guides. Students explain their mission, goals, current performance compared to desired performance, and improvement strategies. Teachers are facilitators, offering additional information when necessary. Traditional schools, however, schedule formal parent-teacher conferences about twice a year. The teacher explains to parents (or other adults) how their child is progressing. Normally, the students are not present at these conferences.

system—An integrated collection of subfunctions that work together to create a greater whole, much like the human body, with its respiratory, digestive, and neurological subsystems (among others) that must work together to make a functioning person. In education, subsystems include teachers and students and all support services, including parents. A related concept is optimization—all processes and activities aligned and pulling together to achieve goals.

Part 1

An Introduction to *The Quality Rubric* and Core Values Underlying the Rubric

INTRODUCTION

At a recent National Quality Education Conference, I was presenting the concepts found in this book to a roomful of educators. I started with a story that went like this:

One of my client superintendents—let's call her Kendra, who has been leading her district forward with quality initiatives for several years now—called me in the middle of the night. She'd just had a nightmare and felt compelled to share her dark dream, hoping also for some reassurance that the portent of the message could be avoided. It seems that in Kendra's nightmare, she found herself speaking with God. No, she didn't dream that she was *God. . . . I recognize this as a common nightmare experienced by many teachers and principals. But rather, Kendra was face-to-face* with *God. The dialogue went like this:*

God: Kendra, what's on your mind, professionally? Any questions you'd like to ask?

Kendra: Well, God, the first thing I'd like to know is . . . will I ever experience a collaborative working relationship with my board members?

God: No, Kendra. Not in your lifetime.

Kendra: Well, okay. What about my building program? Will we be able to have the new facilities we need without community uproar and opposition?

God: No, Kendra. Not in your lifetime.

Kendra (becoming a bit disappointed): God, I've been working so hard these past few years to train all my teachers and administrators in the quality philosophy and quality tools. When will I see evidence that everyone *is implementing these powerful ideas in their classrooms?*

God: Not in my *lifetime, Kendra.*

Now, Kendra realized that *not in God's lifetime* was probably approaching infinity, so she became a bit concerned and decided to call. Out of that discussion was born the idea for *The Quality Rubric,* a simple, practical approach for ensuring that the best strategies adopted by your district are, in fact, completely implemented.

Some of you have probably heard this joke, or some variation of it. I think many of us sometimes feel that we will never see the results of our hard work. In this case, we are talking about transfer of training, implementation, and deployment. How do we ensure that time spent in formal training events (quality tools, CQI, Baldrige, balanced literacy, math problem-solving, or other professional development workshops) transfers into the classroom? Keep reading, because this book has answers for you.

I have been an educator for more than 30 years, working in both public schools and alternative education in the United States and elsewhere. I have been a teacher, curriculum coordinator, and elementary, junior high, and high school principal. I have helped lead many schools with quality improvement initiatives. I have also worked a number of years as an international management development trainer for the health-care industry, in which the focus is often on continuous quality improvement. Like most of you, I've seen "the latest, greatest thing" introduced over and over again in organizations around the world. The cycle is typically one of initial interest among a few leaders, rapid-fire blasts of "training" for the troops, half-hearted deployment in some sections, and eventual abandonment of the new approach. Then the cycle begins anew with the "next greatest thing."

Without doubt, many of the initiatives were well-designed strategies that failed more because of lack of consistent attention to change management principles (DeFeo and Barnard, 2005; Sebastianelli and Tamimi, 2003), especially the concept of "execution" (Bossidy and Charan, 2002). Mankins and Steele (2005, p. 68) present research that documents the breakdown between strategy and performance improvements: "Strategies are approved but poorly communicated. This, in turn, makes the translation of strategy into specific actions and resource plans all but impossible. Lower levels in the organization don't know what they need to do, when they need to do it, or what resources will be required to deliver the performance senior management expects." Another reason for failure is that we tend to view improvement as a series of events, not a process. "Events don't change schools. Long-term ongoing processes change schools" (Lezotte and Pepperl, 1999, p. 31).

I am tired. I guess you are, too. Let's stop the merry-go-round and get off. Let's find an approach that will deliver improved results consistently, an approach that provides a framework for action that can be applied to many different problems. *Let's become single-minded about ensuring 100 percent implementation of our best practices systemwide.* Create, along with your director of quality, an Office of Strategy Management (Kaplan and Norton, 2005) to ensure that strategies and approaches are fully implemented throughout the organization.

The underlying theme of this book is that by accepting a few powerful quality core values and by learning and implementing a few quality tools systematically, you can improve performance in your classroom and school. Your classrooms can become more focused on results, more student centered and student directed, more fun, and more successful. As a school, you can ensure that everyone is implementing the agreed strategies consistently and with fidelity. These improvements can be made with little cost, but you may have to change your attitudes and move away from a teacher-centric classroom model to one in which students take a more active role in decision making. You may need to shift from a principal-centric school leadership model to one that accepts the belief that "all of us are smarter than any one of us." You may have to step outside your gated community and engage your colleagues more openly and in a spirit of team-based continuous improvement.

Quality, also known as total quality management, continuous quality improvement, total quality transformation, Six Sigma, Kaizen breakthrough methodology, and ISO 9000, may be defined as "managing the continuous improvement of service delivery processes and outcomes through data-driven strategies and empowered staff to exceed customer expectations" (Smith, Discenza, and Piland, 1993, p. 35). "Most organizations that implement total quality management, continuous improvement cultures or team systems teach their employees tools to use in reaching decisions and solving problems. Whether these tools have four steps or seven steps, they have four basic components: problem definition, data collection to verify the root cause of the problem, solution generation and action planning, including a mechanism for tracking how well the chosen solution works" (Uhlfelder, 2000, p. 47). Many definitions of quality can be found in the literature, but the following central elements seem always to be present: systems thinking, customer and stakeholder focus, clear goals, results orientation, use of data for decision making, teamwork, use of quality tools, and a commitment to continually improving our processes and outcomes.

This book is designed to simplify some of the most important elements of quality for educators and to place these tools, techniques, and values in a system that can ensure gradual, yet continual, deployment until the entire organization is functioning at a high level. I have steered clear of some of the more complex terminology of quality (split-plot analysis, statistical n control, failure mode and effects analysis, current reality trees) in order to adopt more educator-friendly terms and to limit the scope of this introductory manual.

I must confess that I also wrote this book out of frustration. I have worked with many districts that have invested many thousands of dollars and removed teachers from their classrooms for many hundreds of hours to receive quality training—whether Baldrige in the Classroom, quality tools, or best instructional practices training. Yet, one month, one semester, or one year later, little change has occurred in the culture of the schools, and if no culture change has transpired, you can bet that trend performance results have not improved. Often, islands of experimentation could be observed immediately after training, but teachers and principals soon saw that there were no system-level expectations, no recognition, or no support system to encourage full deployment of the new learning. Huggett (1999, p. 38) warns that

> *Any soft system [such as beliefs and expectations, incentives, supervision, and staff development] that is in conflict with the outcomes you desire will act as a barrier to change. The sooner these systems are identified and aligned, the better. However, conflicting systems not only misdirect behavior, they are often seen by employees as an indication of a lack of resolve or commitment on the part of the leadership team.*

Without clear alignment of these soft systems with your expressed goal for deployment, your new "quality approach" will be put on the shelf along with all those other initiatives, gathering dust communally now.

Look at the nine-box figure (Figure 1.1). One dimension (Y-axis) asks you to reflect on how much quality training your school or district has provided over the past few years. The second dimension (X-axis) asks you to consider the degree of implementation of that training in your school or district. Obviously, nine possibilities exist. For example, box 1 indicates a situation in which very little training (and therefore) very little implementation has occurred. Box 9 suggests an outcome in which much training has been provided and excellent implementation has occurred. Where does your school or district fall among these boxes with respect to quality training or, for that matter, any key initiative, strategy, or approach that you have been attempting to implement? Be honest as you consider this very important question.

My observations, gleaned over the past 10 years of working with education and healthcare organizations as they attempt to implement quality improvement systems, suggest a bleak picture regarding how well we train and how well we implement the training. If responses from a random sampling of organizations were scored and represented in a distribution such as Figure 1.2, the curve would, most likely, be skewed toward the left, with 80%+ of organizations concentrating in boxes 1–6.

Why is there such a poor record regarding implementation of organizational strategies? Because leaders fail to establish the hard and soft systems to ensure that change will take place on a systematic, systemic, and long-term basis. Lezotte and Pepperl advise that after training, educators "should not just come back feeling good about going and then conduct business as usual. A process should be in place whereby teachers come back and plug into an ongoing dialogue that does something with what they've learned. We want a lead-up to the event, then the event itself, and the discussion and implementation to follow it" (1999, p. 31). In *Creating Quality Schools,* the American Association of School Administrators warns that "people are not likely to take new reform efforts [including professional development in quality] seriously unless the district demonstrates its commitment to improvement" (1992, p. 5).

The Quality Rubric provides a process to *ensure that training is transferred into the classrooms and schools— the rubric is a measuring device and a mechanism to project clear expectations for all teachers and administrators that the quality approach will be implemented throughout the learning system.* Combine the ideas in *The*

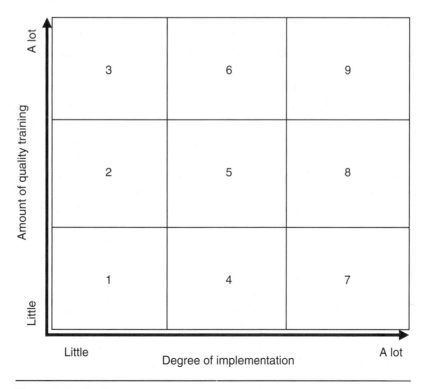

Figure 1.1 Quality survey.

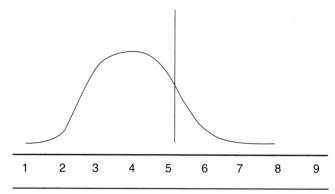

Figure 1.2 Distribution for organizations attempting to implement strategies.

Quality Rubric with solid change management principles (Kotter, 1995; Strebel, 1998) and knowledge of motivation theory (Herzberg, 1966; Gibson, Ivancevich, and Donnelly, 1988) and suddenly, you've increased exponentially your chances of achieving continuous improvement.

The *Baldrige Education Criteria for Performance Excellence* (www.baldrige.nist.gov) stresses the importance of moving logically through two phases en route to improved performance results. Those two phases are (1) identify high-quality strategies or approaches and (2) deploy them systematically for an adequate period of time. The flow here is immutable. You have to progress through the phases (Figure 1.3), much like Covey's (1990) "law of the farm," in which you can't expect to harvest if you haven't prepared the ground and tended to the crops throughout the growing season.

I travel a lot, mostly in my car. National Public Radio helps me pass the time productively. A while ago, I heard a story about the results of a study comparing several diets—all the popular ones you hear so much about. The researchers wanted to know which diet was most effective. They came to the conclusion that, if your goal is simply to lose weight, it probably doesn't matter too much which approach you choose. The key factor in determining one's results seems to have more to do with how consistently the diet is implemented. In other words, do the dieters stick with the program long enough to get the results they desire?

I believe educators are like most dieters. We try a diet for a short time, and when, because of our inconsistency, we fail to achieve results, we proclaim that the diet doesn't work very well. *The Quality Rubric* is designed to help you fully deploy the powerful tools and techniques shown in this book and in others that I mention as resources.

It may be important to state what *The Quality Rubric* is not. This book will *not* provide you with samples of classroom learning rubrics that help teachers know how well students can perform specific skills. There are no writing rubrics (see Flynn and Flynn, 2004, for example), problem-solving rubrics (see http://www.rubrician.com/math.htm, for example), or behavior rubrics (see Marshall and Weisner, 2004, for example). In early reviews of this manuscript, some evaluators expected *The Quality Rubric* to provide such resources for teachers. It does not. This book teaches you about "quality in education" principles and tools and *establishes a rubric that will guide you in logical deployment of these powerful techniques, allowing you to gradually become more and more proficient. The rubric set forth in this book provides administrators and teachers a framework for setting clear expectations for deployment, tracking individual and system growth, and recognizing accomplishments.*

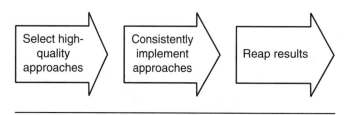

Figure 1.3 Natural flow toward improved results.

After you read *The Quality Rubric,* I hope you will be motivated to start your quality journey—for the kids' sake. Glasser (1990, p. 435) encourages us with these words: "This is what we need to try to do with our students: start early, and talk to them about quality. Give them tools and lots of encouragement. Then stand back and see where they go once the idea of quality education gets inside their heads." Goldberg and Cole (2002, p. 10) advocate that we teach quality to students and begin to view students "as both customers and workers in the educational system." I believe that both suggestions are correct. I have seen the change in students and teachers, once quality takes hold. I hope you will experience the same positive changes.

CORE VALUES AND BELIEFS

Covey (1990) advises that leaders should be directed by principles and that these core beliefs can guide us in the proper direction, even when surrounded by confusing voices. He identifies "lack of shared vision and values" as a chronic organizational problem. Rosenthal and Masarech (2003, p. 4) write that to develop a high-performance culture and organizational success, leaders must purposefully establish

> *shared organizational values that guide employee behavior and influence business practices as your organization delivers on its promises to customers, employees, and other stakeholders. They [values] answer the question, What are your company's guiding principles, its authentic, enduring "rules of the road"? Business strategies will shift; core values do not.*

Core values and beliefs are an integral part of all human endeavors, whether personal or organizational.

There are many lists of core values and hundreds of worthwhile central beliefs that you can use to keep your compass needle pointed in the correct direction. If you do not have a defined (overt) set of values in your organization, begin by interviewing or surveying workers and stakeholders to determine the covert values already in operation. If you become stuck, a simple Web search of "education core values" will yield hundreds of examples that can be reviewed. Professional journals are also a good source of core values. For example, Boggs (2004, p. 43) reports the following list of TQM core values (summarizing previous work by other investigators): visionary leadership, internal and external cooperation, learning, process management, continuous improvement, employee fulfillment, and customer satisfaction. The *Baldrige Education Criteria for Performance Excellence* list 11 core values that are, not surprisingly, similar to those presented by Boggs.

I have identified a number of quality core values as a foundation for this book. Other writers might have selected a somewhat different set of values to emphasize. My list is not intended to be definitive. I simply chose values that align well with the book's purpose, which is stated in the preface.

What are core values, and why are they important? Core values are "anything you feel strongly about that resonates at a deeper level of your being. These are fundamental beliefs that are well-developed and have molded your character for years. . . . When you do something that contradicts these values, your intuition, or gut feeling, will serve as a reminder that something isn't right" (Canfield, Hansen, and Hewitt, 2000, p. 69). Core values should guide thought, talk, and behavior, whether in our personal or organizational lives. By providing my own pared-down list of foundational quality values, I hope to provide an advance organizer for what you will experience in *The Quality Rubric.*

The Quality Rubric is designed to help teachers, staff, principals, and students create learning environments in which the following 10 core values are lived each day.

Personal Accountability for Learning

Each worker in the learning system sees himself or herself as responsible for attaining clear and measurable goals. Quality organizations empower each individual to self-monitor performance and make necessary improvements. "An organization must become a rapid learning organization to continually expand its capacity to do more in the future. Teams need to effectively capture and share knowledge. A rapid learning organization has a cultural norm that promotes rapid learning, sharing and reuse of current knowledge to meet ever changing customer needs" (English and Baker, 2006, p. 44). Implementing such a system has the effect of flattening the organization, speeding better decisions along the pathway toward implementation, improving results, and increasing motivation. Students must "change from behaving as passive recipients of the knowledge offered by the teacher to becoming active learners who can take responsibility for and manage their own learning" (Black, Harrison, Lee, Marshall, and Wiliam, 2004, p. 20). Stiggins (2002, p. 764) suggests that the ultimate goal of student engagement and shared accountability is continual lifelong learning. "Students come to understand what it means to be in charge of their own learning—to monitor their own success and make decisions that bring greater success. This is the foundation of lifelong learning." In a quality system, students, teachers, and principals become responsible for their own devolved list of goals, performance data, and continual improvement.

Crosby (1984) suggests that everyone in an organization adopt a personal commitment to "zero defects" that requires clear focus on performance standards, teamwork to meet high expectations, awareness of nonconformance, and a problem prevention orientation. In such an environment, "high expectations for all" becomes the norm. Garratt (1994, pp. 38–39) writes that learning must be greater than or equal to change, and adopting an attitude that leaders, managers, and workers must engage in "on the shop floor learning" is a symbol of effective management. In a new, more challenging world, learning must be greater than the pace of change if organizations and people are to thrive. Champy (1995, p. 27) suggests that "we have to let go of any feeling of despair about people . . . we must hold fast to our *faith* in human beings: the knowledge and belief that we are all eager to learn, and capable of dedication, high spirits, and individual responsibility" (emphasis in original).

Learning is not only formal learning that takes place in workshops and conferences, but also that which occurs as a result of experience (immersion in the task), reflection (what was noticed), conceptualization (what does it mean), and planning (what will be changed). The learning cycle can be applied to individuals, teams, and organizations (Kolb, 1984). In a quality classroom, expect to see active learning environments in which students are coleaders of their own learning. The commonly heard maxim is that once quality tools, values, and processes are solidly in place, the students should be more tired at the end of the day than the teachers. Compare this vision with reality in many classrooms where "if an alien came from another planet, hovered around a public school, and went back to the home planet to describe what a public school was all about, the alien might say, 'A school is a place where young people go to watch old people work'" (Lezotte and Pepperl, 1999, p. 139).

Alignment

From time to time, we all need the tires on our cars aligned in order to increase tread life, to improve fuel efficiency, and to ensure that the car travels straight down the road toward our goal in the most expeditious manner. When the tires are not aligned, they don't move forward in a parallel fashion, and increased friction is the result.

Most organizations (including schools) need realignment. Repairs require that the school must be clear about its most important goals—something referred to in the quality literature as the dashboard of performance indicators (percentage of students reading on or above grade level, percentage mastering state academic standards, for example). When the dashboard is established with input from all customers and stakeholders, the students, teachers, staff, and principals create their own aligned goals. The dashboard focuses everyone on the key system requirements and outcomes. After performance indicators are clear, strategies (methods for achieving goals) and measures (assessment tools) are aligned across classrooms and among grade levels. There are very few truly aligned schools, and aligned districts are like ivory-billed woodpeckers—we thought there were none, but occasionally someone reports a sighting. Schmoker (1996, p. 21) notes that schools "typically lack clear, common direction and communication that promotes people working toward mutually intelligible goals." His observation regarding poor system alignment reflects the situation in many organizations, not just schools.

Alignment contributes to the development of a common vocabulary and culture, reduces confusion when students and staff move from school to school or from room to room, enhances teamwork, and maximizes scarce resources such as staff development funds and teacher time in the classroom with their students. Alignment leaves room for individual identities, but there must be a common foundation among classrooms and schools in each corporation. "In a quality approach, the school system counts on the cooperative interaction of all its subsystems (individual classrooms and school buildings) for the benefit of the whole system (the district). When subsystems act independently and only in their own best interests, or even in competition with other subsystems, it is called suboptimization" (AASA, 1992, p. 15).

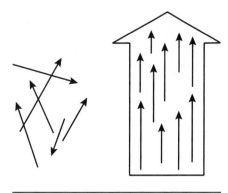

Figure 1.4 The power of alignment.

Note: Inspiration for Figure 1.4 was drawn from a diagram found in the 2006 Baldrige Education Criteria, p. 56, Steps Toward Mature Processes.

In Figure 1.4, the randomly arrayed arrows on the left side of the figure (they look like a game of pick-up-sticks in progress) represent a situation where there is no unifying direction or values. That is quite a contrast with the right side of the figure, where the larger arrow, signifying a strategic plan, mission, core values, and dashboard, unifies and aligns the subelements of the system, just like a magnet would organize metal filings.

When I have shown the "nonaligned and aligned" representations to clients and colleagues in education, healthcare, and not-for-profit organizations, most have commented that their current organizational status approximates the nonaligned graphic. All have indicated a desire to work in more coherent organizations. Randomness and disorganization increase stress and contribute to poor performance. Who among us would purposefully opt for those outcomes?

Continuous Improvement

"Any system, biological, economic, or social, that becomes so encrusted that it cannot self-evolve, a system that systematically scorns experimentation . . . is doomed over the long term" (Meadows, 1999, p. 16). If organizations do not engage in continuous improvement, even in fairly stable environments, gradual decline will be the result. More rapid erosion occurs in today's dynamic environments.

How do we ensure continual growth, as opposed to gradual decline? Institutionalize the continuous quality improvement cycle in your organization and in your life. Plan. Do. Check. Improve. Start anywhere but run through the entire PDCI loop (Figure 1.5). Whether you call it PDCA (McClanahan and Wicks, 1993), PDSA (Byrnes and Baxter, 2005), or PIEI (Bernhardt, 1999), use this powerful tool/organizing principle to make sustained improvement. Action research (Sagor, 2000) is a key companion to the PDCI loop.

The continuous improvement core belief is linked to another important value—personal and organizational learning. Garratt (1994, p. 59) advises that we must "ensure that the organizational climate and culture is developed so that a 'Learning Climate' is encouraged." He further states that there are four prerequisites to establishing an environment in which continuous improvement occurs:

1. All individuals working in an organization must learn "regularly and rigorously from their work."
2. Organizations must establish systems to share the learning.
3. Learning and improvement are valued.
4. The organization "continuously transforms itself through the application of learning."

Garratt's final point provides added justification for *The Quality Rubric,* which was written to help the reader systematically apply a few powerful ideas in order to dramatically change the classroom, school, and district cultures.

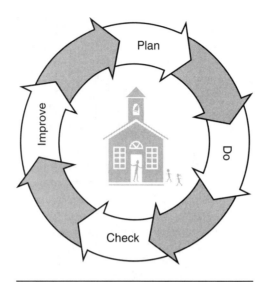

Figure 1.5 The plan, do, check, improve cycle of continuous improvement.

Those who have implemented the continuous improvement core belief find that they now focus on the future rather than the past, and that they do not seek to affix blame for failures. They think, "Okay. We had a failure. How can we learn from this experience?" Continuous improvement also requires that once you achieve goals, you must set higher standards and begin the cycle again on a higher plane.

I worked in a school that needed to improve the process by which students were placed in the correct cars at the end of the day. Before continuous improvement work began, the process required nearly 25 minutes from start to finish. Parent and staff satisfaction with the process was very low. In fact, it would have been easier to measure dissatisfaction, because there was so much more of it. The improvement team checked the causes of poor performance and set an interim goal to reduce the time required to 20 minutes. Within a few weeks, this target had been met, and the team decided to set a higher standard of performance and start the PDCI cycle again. Ultimately, they were able to complete the process (with the same number of cars and kids) in about 12 minutes, and parent satisfaction rose significantly. Quite an improvement!

Data-Driven Decision Making

"Data almost always point to action—they are the enemy of comfortable routines. By ignoring data, we promote inaction and inefficiency" (Schmoker, 1996, p. 33). In a quality improvement environment, data will become some of your most valuable resources. For example, you will use internal performance data to make decisions about future continuous improvement requirements. You will learn to benchmark world-class performers to determine their best practices, and you will become proficient in the use of quality tools such as root cause analysis and time-run charting to help identify opportunities for improvement. Never mind that you may not currently know how to collect and use data effectively. You are not alone. Heritage and Chen (2005, p. 708) write that the likelihood of schools reaching the accountability targets required by state and federal mandates "depends on the ability of educators to collect and analyze data and set goals and targets based on their analysis. Yet the development of these skills has not been a part of most administrator preparation programs and hardly ever has been a feature of preservice or inservice teacher training."

The core value of data-driven decision making requires that you read education research from the most respected journals (*Kappan, Education Leadership, Reading Teacher*) and books like Marzano's *What Work*s series as well as the position statements of national organizations such as the National Council of Teachers of Mathematics. Get in the habit of asking your colleagues, "What data do you have to support that statement (or decision or belief)?"

Continuous quality improvement in your school and classroom must engage all workers and learners, including the students. In fact, *The Quality Rubric* is mostly about teachers learning and implementing techniques and tools that require students to become actively engaged in managing their own learning. Helping students quickly become proficient in the collection, analysis, and use of data for improvement is an important goal of this book. "Kids need to learn to make decisions based on data rather than hunches. They need to look beyond and behind superficial symptoms and surface opinions. They need to dig for the root cause and seek out all pertinent information" (McClanahan and Wicks, 1993, p. 97). Quality tools help students become scientists and problem solvers as they work on issues that directly affect them every day.

One of our schools sought to increase the student attendance rate, hovering at 94.6 percent (when local benchmarks were achieving nearly a 97 percent rate). Improving attendance was a key focus area in the school's improvement plan, and various incentives had been established to reward students for perfect attendance. Nevertheless, interim attendance results were disappointing. Through careful analysis of the data, an improvement team discovered that only 8 percent of students (about 80) were responsible for nearly one-fourth of all missed days (Figure 1.6). The team began to gather data on each of those 80 students in order to determine the root causes of poor attendance. It quickly became clear that the major improvement strategy, a system of rewards (pizza parties, certificates), was not working with these 80 students. After detailed information gathering, including interviews with students, parents, and employers as well as some limited benchmarking, new approaches such as one-on-one mentoring, real-time performance monitoring, and enhanced school-home-school communication were instituted. In short time, the attendance rate rose to interim target levels.

Why all the fuss about data? "Data are to goals what signposts are to travelers; data are not end points, but data are essential to reaching them—the signposts on the road to school improvement" (Schmoker, 1996, p. 30). Without data, we are reduced to random behavior and erratic performance results.

Teamwork

Continuous improvement is best undertaken in a team environment. Two heads are usually better than one. Five or six are even better, if they complement one another in important ways (Belbin, 1993). It is possible to work solo through the elements in *The Quality Rubric,* but the experience will be much more rewarding and effective if you can inspire your colleagues to join you on your journey. Terms such as "nested learning communities" and "communities of practice" (Fink and Resnick, 2001) suggest the importance of merging the concepts of continuous improvement, personal and organizational learning, and teamwork. Powerful improvements can emerge in such an environment. Schmoker (1996, p. 48) notes that "people accomplish more together than in isolation; regular, collective dialogue about an agreed-upon focus sustains commitment and feeds purpose; effort thrives on concrete evidence of progress; and teachers learn best from other teachers." Unfortunately, working in teams is not all that easy. Many teachers have been allowed, and sometimes encouraged, to work alone. They have become

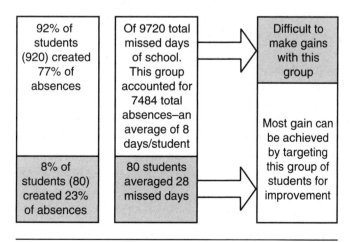

Figure 1.6 How data analysis can help improve performance.

"gated community" educators who open the gate in the morning to allow the students in, then they promptly shut the gate, closing off the classroom until time to leave at the end of the day. Marshall (2005, p. 733) notes the difficulty of getting teachers to work together: "Teachers in the U.S. are accustomed to autonomy, and it takes a tenacious principal to foster this kind of collaboration. It's essential, though, because teams plan better than teachers working solo, and teams generate stronger ideas, provide better support, and increase the likelihood that the supervisory voice will be in each teacher's head. . . ."

And students must also be engaged in teams or cooperative learning groups that identify and solve problems and opportunities for improvement. Not only will teamwork prepare students for the worlds of work and further study, but cooperative grouping also is one of the most effective instructional methods. Marzano, Pickering, and Pollock (2001, p. 87), summarizing several important research studies, report that organizing students in cooperative groups has a powerful effect on learning. The ability to work well in teams is one of the most frequently mentioned skills sought by higher education and employers (Hartman and Feir, 2000; U.S. Department of Labor, 1992), so engaging student teams in solving real classroom, school, and community problems will serve as good preparation for life beyond the pre-K–12 world. As Glasser (1990, p. 432) says, in quality schools students are the workers in the system. Given the correct conditions, students will shift from being passive recipients of knowledge to active constructors of knowledge. "Learning together as a member of a team satisfies the needs for power and for belonging much better than does learning alone. Good lead-managers recognize that, when they can promote and support cooperation among workers, they have laid the foundation for high-quality work."

Results Focus

Unfortunately, "schools have an almost cultural and ingrained aversion to reckoning with, much less living by, results" (Schmoker, 1996, p. 3). But setting goals and making continual progress is motivational—if there is clear focus and alignment around the school and classroom goal set. When teachers talk about "covering material," they are focused on work or processes rather than outcomes. It is important that schools have well-designed processes, but at the end of the day, it's results that count. The results that we are most concerned about are generally of two types: (1) execution of best-practice, evidence-based strategies and (2) interim (leading) and summative (lagging) performance data. Both are critically important if continual improvement is your organization's goal.

I believe that the vast majority of students and teachers go to school each day to pursue the common goal of improving learning results. In quality schools, collaboration groups meet regularly to review the student learning outcomes that have accrued as a result of best-practice processes. Results first; processes second. "We must stop looking at schools in terms of the processes they utilize and start looking at them in terms of the results they are getting. For the last 100 years, we've judged schools as being good or bad based on inputs and processes. Regional accreditation programs have asked schools to extensively document their processes—how many books are in the school library, what is the amount of square feet in the science lab, etc.? They never confronted the question of whether the children were learning what it is we want them to know and do!" (Lezotte and Pepperl, 1999, p. 88). This focus on process rather than results is one of the reasons that schools dabble in one "fad" after another. Quality organizations are concerned with processes only as a vehicle that delivers improved results. If the process does not deliver, it is improved or jettisoned.

Maintain a constant focus on your dashboard performance indicators. Work hard, because without effort, nothing is achieved. Celebrate successes, because as Bossidy and Charan (2002, p. 92) suggest, if an organization "rewards and promotes people for execution, its culture will change."

In quality schools, educators sometimes complain that continuous improvement is hard work, and the work never seems to be finished. Both statements are true. However, you are rewarded for your continuous improvement efforts in the form of happier, more successful students and colleagues.

High Expectations

Studies have shown that you get what you expect (Rosenthal and Jacobson, 1968). If you set low expectations for students, teachers, staff, principals, and schools (either intentionally or unintentionally), don't be surprised when you get poor performance. Work to establish a culture of high expectations. Examine your practices, statements, and beliefs. Begin to weed out all things that contribute to a culture of low expectations. Good and Brophy (1987, pp. 152–153), following a review of the "expectations literature," summarize by saying, "teachers' attitudes and expectations about different students can lead them to treat the students differently, sometimes to the extent of producing self-fulfilling prophecy effects. A particular danger is that low expectations combined with an attitude of futility will be communicated to certain students, leading to erosion of their confidence and motivation for school learning." Obviously, I hope you will remain on the other side of this argument. Have positive attitudes for all students, and set consistently high expectations.

> *"If we are not here to promote the success of all students, then why are we here? We are not here to promote only the education of those who are easy to teach, who speak English fluently, who fit school in between before-school athletics and after-school fine arts, who are clean and well fed, or who behave nicely every day . . . We are here to promote the success of all students."* (Wilmore, 2002, p. 19) (emphasis in original)

Many of your students have come to you with dangerously low reserves of self-esteem and self-confidence. Covey (1990) would say their emotional bank accounts are empty. Meadows (1999) explains how inflows and outflows into systems affect the standing stock or reserves of whatever is deemed important to the system. For too many of your students, all their stocks of confidence and esteem have been drained, and experiences at school are not providing any new positive inflows that might gradually improve their fortunes. Many of the approaches outlined in *The Quality Rubric* can help these students experience success. Success, even modest success, can begin to plant seeds of hope. Hope leads to more effort. Effort leads to improvement. Improvement leads to more hope. Often, this improvement cycle is kick-started by an adult who consistently expresses high expectations for others (Figure 1.7).

Lezotte and Pepperl (1999, p. 109) write that in effective schools, "there is a climate of high expectations in which the staff believes and demonstrates that all students can attain mastery of the essential school skills. Further, the staff members believe they have the capability to help all students attain that mastery" and "high expectations for the learner must be launched from a platform of the teacher first having high expectations for self."

Figure 1.7   Critical connections for success.

Quality educators find ways to build student self-esteem through increased student learning. Improved learning is the tide that can float all ships.

High expectations are also important for adult workers in the system—the teachers, administrators, and support staff who are expected to lead the way with deployment of quality attitudes and tools. *The Quality Rubric* sets forth the rationale that without clear expectations and a system for tracking and recognizing growth, staff will not implement "quality in education" systematically or systemically. Leaders must rise to this challenge. "Quality doesn't happen when high standards are set. It happens when leaders consistently enforce and reward these standards" (Surplus, 2000, p. 60). In other words, just saying that you would like to see quality in each classroom won't get the job done. You also have to express high expectations for implementation, monitor activities, and recognize growth.

Focus on the Vital Few

Juran is often credited with the phrase "vital few," although the roots of this concept have been traced back much earlier (Phillips-Donaldson, 2004). This important idea—that of focusing on a few very important goals or pieces of data—is also called the Pareto rule or the 80/20 principle. Koch writes (1998, p. 17) that "a majority of any phenomenon will be explained or caused by a minority of the actors participating in the phenomenon. Eighty percent of the results come from 20 percent of the causes. A few things are important; most are not." Carefully select a few most important performance indicators such as percentage of students reading and writing on or above grade level, and relentlessly pursue breakthrough performance in these areas. Don't dilute your efforts by juggling too many initiatives. This advice is especially true when considering whole school improvement. "Even more than in a classroom, the success of a genuine school improvement effort requires selecting and maintaining a clear long-term focus on a few important priorities" (Wagner, 1998, p. 514). When you've done your homework and selected good strategies designed to close the gap in performance, stick with them until you achieve success. The very best strategy, if only partially implemented, will yield limited results. But fully implement a moderately good strategy, and your results will probably be superior to most schools.

In education organizations, 80 percent of effectiveness comes from focusing on 20 percent of the possible goals (reading and writing first and foremost). Once you've narrowed your focus to a few goals, devote 80 percent of your resources (time, staff, and money) to achieving success, and growth will occur. (See Figure 1.8.) Lezotte and Pepperl (1999, p. 128) write about the power of focusing on a few vital improvement strategies: "I believe, and my experience so far tells me, if we can get a school to do a few things and do them with fidelity and with some depth, we're going to get a higher yield than if we scramble 1,000 different ideas."

In our personal lives, many of us create lists of important tasks that must be accomplished—often on busy Saturdays. Let's say you have 10 items on your list. All are important. All must be accomplished eventually. Focusing on the vital few means that we should identify the one or two most important jobs among the 10 and spend as

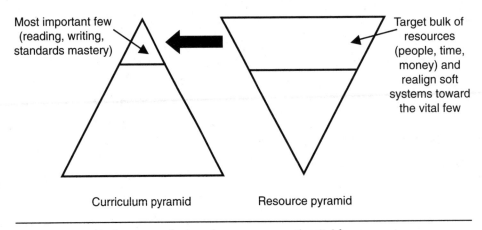

Figure 1.8 Achieving success by focusing resources on the vital few.

much time as is necessary to accomplish those two tasks. If successful, we will achieve at least an 80 percent "happiness" or "satisfaction" result from our efforts. On the other hand, if we move down the list in random fashion, at the end of the day, we may find that we accomplished several "lower level" tasks, but the most important work was left uncompleted. In this situation, our personal satisfaction with our efforts will not approach the 80 percent level. The simple secret to success is knowing what is most important and targeting effort and resources at accomplishing those few goals.

Leadership

In a quality organization, leadership is practiced at all levels. Students are the leaders of their own learning systems. The same is true for teachers in their classrooms, for support staff in their functional areas, and for principals and leadership teams at the school level. Champy (1995, p. 3) argues for system changes such that "responsibility and authority are so widely distributed throughout the organization that virtually everyone becomes a manager, if only of his or her own work." Covey (1990) advises that we master personal leadership first by ensuring that our actions are congruent with our beliefs and principles. Once we have our internal houses in order, allowing us to talk and act consistently from a solid core value base, we can then begin to influence others at the interpersonal, managerial, and organizational levels (Covey, 1990; Napolitano and Henderson, 1998). "Leadership can come from anywhere at anytime if people are given the skills and the expectation. Gaining the involvement and commitment of the culture requires that leadership be intentionally developed in every area of the organization" (Ray and Bronstein, 2001, p. 82).

Remember that the best way to lead is to model the way. Walk the talk. Continually communicate your vision, core beliefs, and goals. Demonstrate your ability to engage in continuous improvement. Share success data to show that quality improvement works. Constantly look for ways to reinforce movement in the right direction. Redirect when people stray. And if you are the principal or superintendent, remember that in modern, high-performing organizations, leadership is ubiquitous. It is not a position on an organizational chart. "It's still important for the principal to be the instructional leader, but because of the nature of organizational changes going on all around us, the concept of leadership is much more dispersed. The evolution of the role of the principal is now more to become the leader of leaders, rather than the leader of followers. What we have is collaborative leadership, with teachers becoming more empowered" (Lezotte and Pepperl, 1999, p. 108). In a more detailed reading of Lezotte and Pepperl, it becomes clear that they would include student leadership and student accountability and responsibility for learning results along with teacher and administrative leadership. "School leadership needs to be redistributed in ways that share responsibilities across the school community and that value collaborative decision making" (Neuman and Simmons, 2000, p. 10).

Systems Thinking

When explaining the concept of a system, I often start with a physiological example of the human body as a wholly integrated collection of subsystems. Most people have had at least some experience in this area (health class or visits to physicians). I ask participants to identify some of the important human subsystems. Although there are many varied classification approaches in the medical and scientific literature, participants generally list the respiratory, digestive, and neurological functions and then struggle somewhat to identify others, such as the musculoskeletal and immune systems. But the point has been made. If each of us is to function at peak performance levels "on the whole," our subsystems must also be operating effectively independently and in tandem with all other components.

Organizations can also be thought of as systems. "As a single system a school district is made up of an interconnected set of components, forces, and relationships working together toward a common aim or purpose" (AASA, 1992, p. 8). If each subsystem (e.g., classroom teachers, students, parents, secretaries, administrators, librarians) is working effectively as a unit and in collaboration with other subsystems, the overall organization will be able to achieve high levels of performance. If one or more subsystems falter, overall performance will be affected in myriad ways.

When considering subsystem operational enhancements, quality thinkers know that they must consider all the ways changes will affect other system elements. Prevette (2003, pp. 32–33) asks, "Why do we lament that the whole is less than the sum of the parts? It is because we tend not to work on the whole but only on the parts. Systems thinkers, instead, focus on the whole, paying attention to the interactions between the parts rather than the parts themselves."

Yamashita and Spataro (2004, p. 17) write that we must look at the "organization as a living organism that needs to be fed, inspired, protected, and nourished. To make a healthy organism, you have to put its fundamental systems into balance so the parts are working with each other rather than against each other. Organizations that are out of balance become stuck—unable to move forward." In quality-minded organizations, every worker (teachers, students, staff) knows his/her goals, current performance results, key processes, and how the work being performed integrates with activities and goals of others so that the entire system can be optimized.

> *"Schools that learn and improve are those that approach change from a systems perspective (Senge et al., 2000). The more systemic the change, the more the school embodies change in behaviors, culture, and structure, and the more lasting the change will be."* (Goldberg and Cole, 2002, p. 9)

If success is the goal, your organization (classroom, work area, school) must be managed effectively. A proper management system requires a number of interdependent components, shown in Figure 1.9. Each of the components shown in the Collaborative, Inquiry-Based Systems Model is vitally important, and if one area is performing poorly or lacks alignment with the others, overall results will be negatively affected.

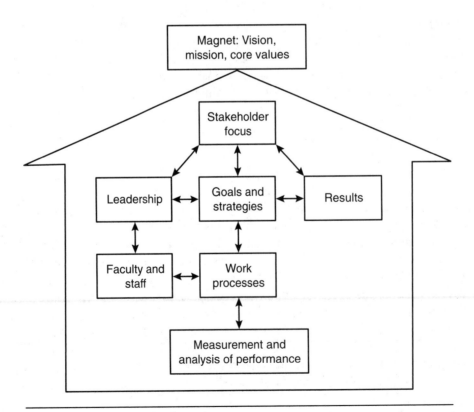

Figure 1.9   Collaborative, inquiry-based systems model.
Based on 2005 Baldrige Criteria.

As a common beginning point, an organization gathers fresh knowledge about its stakeholders and their needs (Stakeholder Focus Box) and translates this information into performance indicators (Goals and Strategies Box/Results Box). But before proper goals and strategies can be finalized, leaders and faculty (Leadership Box/Faculty and Staff Box) gather data about current and past performance as well as that of world-class performers (Measurement and Analysis of Performance Box/Results Box). For example, after listening to a wide range of stakeholders, the school learns that "all students reading on or above grade level" is a key expectation. Percentage of students reading on or above grade level becomes a performance indicator (at the top of the curriculum pyramid, Figure 1.8). At this point, faculty members review current and past performance data. Perhaps they learn that generally, only about 60 percent of their students read at expected levels. They may also learn that schools similar to theirs have made dramatic improvements, achieving an overall rate of 80 percent to 90 percent of students reading on or above grade level. They then write a goal (increase the percentage of students reading on or above grade level from 60 percent to 85 percent in three years as measured by running records and leveled books). Because they know of schools where improved performance has been achieved, a team of administrators and teachers visit in order to learn about the methods (Work Processes Box/Strategies Box) used by staff (Faculty and Staff Box). Once these new approaches have been carefully reviewed and selected for implementation, faculty receive training (Faculty and Staff Box), and leadership and coaches (Leadership Box) provide ongoing evaluation and support as interim reading performance growth is checked frequently (Measurement and Analysis of Performance). The school leaders adjust action plans (Goals and Strategies Box) based on reviews of faculty and student performance. As a result of this and other work various improvement teams perform, the school refreshes its mission to read: Our mission is to teach all students to read and write and to master the state standards in all subjects. Note that this mission is limited in scope and very specific (and ultimately measurable), unlike many that hang on schools' walls. Also, the school resets its vision to read: In three years or less, 85 percent of our students will read on or above grade level, and we will be the highest performing school in our district. Finally, the school establishes a new core belief that "all students can learn to read, given the right kind of support." Leadership and faculty regularly check hard and soft systems to ensure they are in alignment with this core belief (see Kaplan and Norton, 2005, for example).

In quality-minded schools where alignment work has occurred, the team has established clear goals (all students will read on or above grade level) and strategies (Balanced Literacy), and staff development can be aligned with strategies (100 percent of staff will be trained in and be expected to fully implement Balanced Literacy). Processes and job aids (rubrics) have been established to help teachers know exactly how to implement Balanced Literacy, and coaches and administrators can use these same rubrics to ensure uniform, correct deployment. There are many other connections, and you can refer to the *Baldrige Education Criteria for Performance Excellence* for more detail.

CORE VALUES: SO WHAT?

I've worked in and with many organizations that have developed lists of core values and beautifully written vision and mission statements. People often wonder how such arcane concepts as visions, missions, and core values can ever impact day-to-day operations. In most organizations, the simple answer is, "They don't."

The reason for their lack of impact is often related to the fact that measurement and followthrough have not been considered. Mission statements, for example, often include terms such as "create lifelong learners" or "develop the full potential of each of our students." These are, on the surface, laudable aims. However, achievement of these aims cannot be measured. You need to back away from a concept such as "lifelong learner" and identify linked, prerequisite subskills and associated measures that can provide the organization with data and input for program design and continual improvement.

Core values can be equally slippery. When thinking about core values, your mind should immediately shift to thoughts of "What would this value sound like and look like in action? How would I know if we are living this value in my classroom, school, and district?" In a later section, I have shown how to develop a core values matrix that will help students learn what the value means and how they will be able to demonstrate it regularly in your classroom. A similar matrix can be developed for the school. As you begin to "live" the 10 core beliefs of *The*

Table 1.1 Practical methods of demonstrating *The Quality Rubric's* core values.

Core value	Short definition/clarifying information	Examples in *The Quality Rubric* (tools, techniques, concepts that operationalize the core value)
Personal accountability for learning	Each person (teacher, staff member, administrator, student) accepts responsibility for achieving learning and improvement goals. Learning occurs in typical environments such as classrooms and in continuous improvement teams.	Data folders, learning process, student-led conferences, S2S talks
Alignment	People work together around common goals and use common processes and measures in order to improve effectiveness and efficiency.	Mission statements, dashboard, strategic planning, S2S talks, collaborative work teams, core beliefs, stakeholder matrix, process flowcharts, evidence-based best practices
Continuous improvement	Manage the continuous improvement of processes and results through data-driven approaches and teams to meet or exceed stakeholder and customer requirements.	PDSA/PDCA/PDCI cycle, learning process, Classroom and School Quality Rubrics, continuous improvement team projects and brochures, quality tools, benchmarking, process flowcharts
Data-driven decision making	Use data and information, including measurement results and research, to choose the best responses to opportunities for improvement.	Dashboard, aligned measures throughout the system, quality tools, benchmarking, S2S talks, classroom displays of data, data folders
Teamwork	Teams are collections of individuals with complementary skills whose mission is to achieve specific goals.	Continuous quality improvement teams, process flowcharts, benchmarking, stakeholder matrix, mission statements, core beliefs, strategic planning, dashboard
Results focus	Accept the importance of learning and performance outcomes as the key measures of organizational success.	Dashboard, SMART goals, continuous improvement, student-led conferences, data folders, stakeholder matrix
High expectations	Establish a culture in which every worker strives to reach targets, and when targets are achieved, raise the bar and continue progressing. Believe and act as if all students can meet learning goals, given enough time and resources.	Benchmarking, stakeholder matrix, student-led conferences, continuous improvement process, data folders, 100% goals
Focus on the vital few	Focus the organization on the few most important goals, and adopt a few powerful strategies to achieve those goals. Relentlessly pursue success in a limited number of key performance areas.	Dashboard, Pareto exercises and use of other quality tools, evidence-based best practices, strategic planning, S2S talks, stakeholder matrix, mission statements, data folders
Leadership	Establish a vision of success, and organize the system in such a way that success is achieved. Take responsibility for continual improvement at one's own level in the organization.	Mission statements, core beliefs, dashboard, strategic planning, student-led conferences, S2S talks
Systems thinking	Realize that complex systems are composed of many interrelated subsystems and that effectiveness comes when all subsystems work in harmony and at high levels. Poor performance in one area affects the whole.	Stakeholder matrix, Classroom and School Quality Rubrics, S2S talks, dashboard, strategic planning

Quality Rubric, as well as others that you and your colleagues deem important, you may want to complete the activities in the "Core Beliefs" section at one of your next staff development opportunities. Continue to seek ways to "walk and talk" your values.

In Table 1.1, I have demonstrated how *The Quality Rubric's* 10 core values are reflected in this book's tools and techniques.

ORGANIZATION OF *THE QUALITY RUBRIC*

The Quality Rubric is a practical book that will provide you with the information and tools necessary to *begin your quality journey through four increasingly challenging performance levels.* Part 1 has introduced a few key quality concepts to the reader, provided some background about why *The Quality Rubric* was written, and helped connect important core beliefs with the tasks contained in the rubrics. Part 2 of the book is oriented toward the classroom. Part 3 of *The Quality Rubric* focuses briefly on school-level implementation.

Both the Classroom Quality Rubric (page 19) and the School Quality Rubric (page 73) can be adjusted by adding items to each level, deleting tasks, or rearranging items if you see a more natural flow. Your school and district may also choose to adjust vocabulary that I have used to fit more closely with your experience. *The concept I am attempting to explain is one of gradual implementation of quality training in your school, with clear expectations that eventually, all staff will be operating at a Quality Level 4, or higher.*

I have laid out *The Quality Rubric* in a format that provides a logical flow for the work that must be accomplished. You will see that I begin by having you identify your customers and their needs; develop mission statements and lists of core values; establish the dashboard; collect data; use quality tools to help along the way, especially in gathering performance data and analyzing root causes of failures; set goals and plans, collaborate around data; and use the information for continuous improvement. The various sections follow this simple step-by-step approach and will guide you to your goals.

Finally, you may feel after reading *The Quality Rubric* that "this is all very nice, but I have to teach my standards." At the end of several sections, I've included a list of common math and language arts standards that will be supported by incorporation of quality tools and continuous improvement activities in your classrooms. For example, many states require that students learn to "represent data on a number line and in tables, including frequency tables" and to "deliver persuasive arguments including evaluation and analysis of problems and solutions and causes and effects." By teaching students how to maintain their own personal data folders and to lead their own parent-teacher-student conferences, you will be helping them apply the standards to real-world activities. Quality tools, techniques, and core values can *help* you teach your standards, and everyone will have fun!

I will close Part 1 of *The Quality Rubric* with a positive quotation from McClanahan and Wicks, two of the earliest advocates of quality in classrooms:

> *After using these tools in your class, not only will you notice a natural, evolutionary change in your own teaching style, you'll also notice a change in your students. Why? Because facilitative leadership breeds facilitative behaviors. As your kids become more and more comfortable with the tools and techniques, they'll begin to take more and more initiative to facilitate effective performance in the classroom. Initiative isn't a personality trait, but rather a matter of know-how (1993, p. 147).*

I hope you are excited about moving through *The Quality Rubric* levels. If you are successful, you *and* your students will benefit.

Part 2

The Classroom Quality Rubric and Explanation of Key Elements

ABOUT RUBRICS

Before you examine the specific aspects of the Classroom Quality Rubric, I'd like to discuss the purposes of rubrics as well as some of their characteristics.

First, what does the word *rubric* mean? I know when I first heard it seven or eight years ago, I was a bit confused. Checking the typical dictionary doesn't help much. The *Merriam-Webster Dictionary* explains that a rubric is "an authoritative rule of conduct or procedure." I suppose for educators, this definition is somewhat on target. An educator-friendly explanation that many may be familiar with is the one supplied by Stevens and Levi (2005, p. 3) in their book, *Introduction to Rubrics.* Stevens and Levi write that "at its most basic, a rubric is a scoring tool that lays out the specific expectations for an assignment. Rubrics divide an assignment into its component parts and provide a detailed description of what constitutes acceptable or unacceptable levels of performance for each of those parts." Although there are many definitions of the construct, most definitions include "performance criteria," "self-evaluation," and "consistency" as key elements. "In its simplest form, the rubric includes a task description (the assignment), a scale of some sort (levels of achievement, possibly in the form of grades), the dimensions of the assignment (a breakdown of the skills/knowledge involved in the assignment), and descriptions of what constitutes each level of performance (specific feedback) all set out on a grid" (Stevens and Levi, 2005, pp. 5–6).

Rubrics are designed to help educators evaluate and give helpful feedback to learners on complex performance tasks such as writing or problem solving—areas in which multiple-choice or true/false type assessments are found wanting. Rubrics are helpful because they provide detailed information about behaviors, skills, and knowledge that must be demonstrated in order to reach certain levels of performance. For example, if you want to reach Quality Level 4 as outlined in this book's rubric (Table 2.1), you can review the performance criteria for that and previous levels, read the material in the book, and align your activities in such a way as to achieve the desired outcome. So, rubrics are instructional as well as evaluative tools. By clearly specifying the expectations for performance, rubrics help us achieve consistency across learners. And you can be fairly confident that colleagues will have more or less the same experiences. Rubrics that make use of constructed-response assessment specify "high-quality performance criteria that help us focus in on the most telling aspects of performance and be consistent with one another" (Arter and McTighe, 2001, p. 3).

Good and Brophy (1987, p. 314), although not using the term *rubric,* discuss the importance of goals, performance appraisals, and self-reinforcement when they suggest that educators and students need "help in assessing progress toward established goals by using *appropriate standards for judging levels of success.* In particular, they need to learn to compare their work with absolute standards or with their own previous performance levels rather than with the performance levels of others" (emphasis in original).

The Quality Rubric is your guide to systematic and sustained progress toward implementation of the quality tools and philosophy found in this and other continuous improvement books. It is your companion and your road map. *The Quality Rubric* provides a clear picture of a desired destination, and you can use it to communicate goals and intentions to others so you won't have to journey alone.

Table 2.1 Classroom quality rubric.

Accomplish each task in a level. Seek certification by your peers. Move on to the next level and repeat. Celebrate as you and your colleagues move through the levels.

Category	Accomplishments
Quality Level 1	• Completed customer/stakeholder matrix • Facilitated student-generated classroom and personal mission statements • Developed core beliefs matrix • Established your beginning dashboard of performance indicators • Created student data folders aligned with your beginning dashboard • Developed teacher data folder for above
Quality Level 2	• Completed customer/stakeholder matrix • Facilitated student-generated classroom and personal mission statements • Developed core beliefs matrix • Established a more developed dashboard of performance indicators • Created student data folders aligned with more developed dashboard • Developed teacher data folder for above • Implemented student-led conferences • Flowcharted one classroom process • Conducted quarterly S2S meetings with principal
Quality Level 3	• Completed customer/stakeholder matrix • Facilitated student-generated classroom and personal mission statements • Developed core beliefs matrix • Established a fully developed dashboard of performance indicators • Created student data folders aligned with fully developed dashboard • Developed teacher data folder for above • Implemented student-led conferences • Flowcharted three classroom processes • Conducted quarterly S2S meetings with principal • Demonstrated use of three quality tools for classroom improvement • Participated in at least one benchmarking visit or best-practice identification team • Completed brochure documenting continuous improvement project that delivered improved student learning results or a process Improvement with supporting data
Quality Level 4	• Completed customer/stakeholder matrix • Facilitated student-generated classroom and personal mission statements • Developed core beliefs matrix • Established a fully developed dashboard of performance indicators • Created student data folders aligned with fully developed dashboard • Developed teacher data folder for above • Implemented student-led conferences • Flowcharted five classroom processes • Conducted quarterly S2S meetings with principal • Demonstrated use of five quality tools for classroom improvement • Participated in at least two benchmarking visits or best-practice identification teams • Completed two brochures documenting continuous improvement projects that delivered improved student learning results or process improvements with supporting data • Developed classroom, grade-level, or subject-area strategic plan • Conducted monthly S2S meetings with students • Conducted quarterly celebrations of performance achievement/ progress

A detailed explanation of each of the tasks listed in the Classroom Quality Rubric can be found in this book, along with examples.

A word about "certification." By certification, I mean formally acknowledging completion of the activities in each level according to your rubric. You can "self-certify" or you can team with another teacher to endorse each other's achievements. Grade-level teams of teachers can collaborate and support one another. When your classroom feels ready to be certified, invite a knowledgeable colleague in to review what you've accomplished and to provide feedback. Schools can also develop quality coaches who are available for mentoring and certification visits—when teachers are ready. You can print certificates (like the one shown in Appendix C) for display in classrooms in order to acknowledge the excellence demonstrated by you and your students. There is nothing authoritative or evaluative (in the normal sense of that word) about the certification process. It's just teachers helping teachers and students get better.

Remember that *The Quality Rubric* stresses continuous improvement. If we, as adults, are unwilling to let others critique our work and to strive for higher and higher levels of performance, what model are we providing for our students who are exposed to evaluation multiple times each day? And what does that say about our profession?

Start slowly and pick up speed once you see how effective these methods can be.

In the next pages, you will find short sections devoted to each of the quality tools/activities listed in the Classroom Quality Rubric, along with examples and forms that can be used to quick-start the process of implementing quality education in your classrooms and schools. Let's begin with developing a customer matrix.

CUSTOMER AND STAKEHOLDER MATRIX

The *Baldrige Education Criteria for Performance Excellence* features "stakeholder focus" prominently. In fact, it is arguably the starting point for system design and all improvement activities within a systems model. Without a clear understanding of stakeholder requirements, quality improvement activities run the risk of being misguided. Listening to the "voice of the customer" (Becker, 2005; Wallace, 1999) ensures that we have the proper starting point for alignment of all other aspects of the systems model.

Begin by developing a customer matrix, also known as a stakeholder matrix. Many educators are uncomfortable with the concept of "customer" (at least in the beginning), so use "stakeholder" if you wish. Remember that customer usually means someone directly receiving services or products of the system (students, teachers), while stakeholders may be a bit more removed but still very interested in the effectiveness of your system (society, employers). "A school system provides knowledge and learning experiences analogous to an industrial or commercial system's products and services. For a school, the product is knowledge, and the services are learning experiences" (Stimson, 2003, p. 38). The business world looks to customers for information about needs that they then hope to satisfy in the quest for profits. In education, we think of students, parents, business, and higher education (Hartman and Feir, 2000) as some initial customers and stakeholders who expect that schools will develop students who are able to read, write, calculate and solve problems, work well in teams, and on and on.

To develop your matrix, "identify the key 'customers' at all levels in the education system. List their requirements and design your system to meet and exceed their needs" (AASA, 1992, p. 29). Begin by engaging the students in a brainstorming discussion of the following questions:

1. Who should care that we do well in school?
2. What do those people expect of us?
3. How can we check to be sure that we know their needs?

By starting with a clear understanding of stakeholder needs, you can be sure that you've got the correct goal focus. Organizational and individual efforts wouldn't be worth much if we achieved some goals but no one cared because they weren't the correct goals. Covey (1989) advises us that we should "begin with the end in mind," and identification of stakeholder needs is the first step along that path. All quality improvement work must begin (What do you need?) and end (Did we successfully provide for your needs?) with the stakeholder. Needs assessments, customer matrixes, interviews, and questionnaires are useful quality tools for identifying (front-end) needs and expectations as well as (back-end) satisfaction levels.

Use the information gathered from questions 1 and 2 to help the students write their classroom missions and personal goals that will be placed in their data folders (see page 33).

Understanding that other people have a stake in whether learners and schools are successful is an important realization for students. Glasser (1990, p. 429) suggests that "for workers, including students, to do high-quality work, they must be managed in a way that convinces them that the work they are asked to do satisfies their needs. The more it does, the harder they will work."

A few years ago, a school that was beginning its quality journey invited area employers, a parent, a college admissions adviser, a military recruiter, and local entrepreneurs to talk to students about knowledge, skills, and attitudes the graduates would need. The students listened carefully, asked good questions, took notes, and incorporated the information into their class mission statement, core values, and personal goals. Suddenly, a lot of the things they were learning in school took on added importance. This "checking with the customers" step was added to the school's strategic planning process, thereby ensuring regular input from key stakeholders.

Adjust the detail of the matrix as students mature. At the elementary level, the customers/stakeholders are probably students, parents, and the current-level and next-grade-level teachers. In middle and high school you can add current and future employers, postsecondary institutions, and society. Tables 2.2, 2.3, and 2.4 contain three sample matrixes—elementary and secondary student examples and a matrix created by a teacher.

Academic Standards Supported by These Activities:

- Ask questions for clarification and understanding.
- Report on a topic with facts and details, drawing from several sources of information.
- Use various reference materials, including online resources.
- Support opinions with researched, documented evidence and with visual displays.

PERSONAL AND CLASSROOM MISSION STATEMENTS

Clarifying and aligning purpose can help improve performance among a wide range of indicators. "Living your purpose requires single-mindedness—a resolve to do whatever it takes. . . . It inflames a deep passion and creates a feeling of significance. When your purpose is clear, your life will have meaning" (Canfield, Hansen, Hewitt, 2000, p. 276).

Schmoker (1996, p. 18) faults schools for "the gap between the need—and intent—to improve academic performance in our schools on the one hand, and the conspicuous and virtual absence of clear, concrete academic goals in most school or district planning efforts on the other. Without explicit learning goals, we are simply not set

---

Table 2.2 Elementary student customer/stakeholder matrix.

Student name: *Wanda*		Grade level: 3	
Who cares?	**What is expected?**	**How do we know?**	**Personal and class goals**
Myself	Learn to read, write, do well in math. Pass our tests. Treat each other nicely. Come to school each day I'm not sick. Behave. Have fun.	We had a class discussion about what we all want, and we listed all the ideas on the board.	Pass all my tests in all my classes. Increase my reading level from H to M by the end of the year. Increase my writing level from 5 to 6. Don't act up and get a yellow or red.
Other kids in the class	They all want mostly the same stuff, but they also talked about us treating each other nice and not making anyone feel bad. No making fun of one another.	We talked about this a looonnng time in class. I didn't know that sometimes we hurt each other's feelings even without thinking.	Never make anyone feel bad. If someone makes me feel bad, I will tell her, and we can talk about it so it doesn't happen again.
Mom and Grandma	Pretty much the same things. They wanted me to put down "be safe at school" and "be nice to my teachers and bus driver" too.	I asked them to look at the list we made to see if we missed anything.	Not get sent to the office for being bad. Be nice to all people each day. Don't get hurt at school.
Fourth-grade teachers	Know my adding and subtracting facts. Get all our homework turned in on time.	They looked at our list and came to our room to talk to us.	Get 100% on my math facts tests. Get all greens for homework.
Mrs. Jones, my third-grade teacher	Learn to read and write better. Master my facts. Be good. Have fun.	We asked her during our first class meeting of the year.	Same

Table 2.3   Secondary student customer/stakeholder matrix.

Student name: *Richard*   **Grade level: 11**

Who cares?	What is expected?	How do we know?	Personal and class goals
Myself	Passing grades, improved writing, homework turned in. I also want to learn a second language because I'm interested in international finance as a career. Take the right classes so I can get an Academic Honors Diploma next year. Safe school.	We brainstormed in groups of five and then shared our thoughts as a class. We also did an Internet search to get ideas. The key words we used were "education outcomes" and "education goals."	Pass all my tests and all my classes for sure and maintain a 3.5 GPA because I want to try for a scholarship. Homework turned in on time. Increase my writing ability so I can do an independent research paper of 5–7 pages. Good attendance and behavior. Do my part to keep the school safe. Get good grades in Spanish.
My parents	They agreed with what I had written for my goals. They included "begin to learn about college options, including financing."	I asked them to look at the list we made and see if we missed anything.	Meet with the counselor. Learn about ways to finance college. Do Internet searches for good international finance programs. Schedule some college visits.
Universities	Very good writing skills and group presentation skills. Ability to organize and meet deadlines without much adult help. Research skills. Ability to work with lots of different people.	I e-mailed seven universities that have finance programs, and they wrote back with really similar information.	Take every chance offered to make presentations. Make friends with José and practice my Spanish. Travel to Mexico with the Spanish club.

Table 2.4   Mr. Hayden's customer/stakeholder matrix.

Teacher name: *Carl Hayden*   **Grade level: 6 (Math)**

Who cares?	What is expected?	How do we know?	Personal and class goals
My students	Learn about math, have fun, not too much homework, safe place, don't flunk the course	Class affinity and consensograms activities the first few days of each semester	100% of my students achieve at least a 75% score in my class. We will have no discipline referrals. Homework rates will remain above my three-year average of 98%. Weekly plus/delta will show enjoyment of learning.
Myself	High levels of student academic success, satisfaction with learning activities, regular attendance, student responsibility and initiative, good behavior	I've taught 12 years, and these are minimum performance indicators if we are all going to have a successful year.	100% of my students achieve at least a 75% score in my class. Attendance rate in my class will be at least as high as the school average. We will have no discipline referrals. Homework rates will remain above my three-year average of 98%. Weekly plus/delta will show enjoyment of learning.
Seventh-grade teachers	They also stressed that too many students don't know basic math facts.	During collaboration time, we discuss needs. Also, our test data from last year highlight this problem.	100% of students will pass a math facts proficiency test by the end of the course.
State DOE	Mastery of our state's academic standards	State's website	100% of students will pass the state test in math.
Parents	Better communication about homework and grade averages	I send a short questionnaire to the parents of all my students at the beginning of each semester.	Establish a web page to show homework assignments so parents can check from home.

up and organized for improvement, for results. Only such goals will allow us to analyze, monitor, and adjust practice toward improvement." Goals, missions, and purposes are intertwined, providing necessary direction for improvement efforts.

Once the customer/stakeholder matrix is completed by each student, you are ready to help turn the information they've gathered into a personal mission statement or purpose statement. Instruct students to look at the goals they've written in the right-hand column. Find the most important goals and write a mission that looks like the two examples shown on pages 25–26 (using Wanda and Richard's information). I have provided a teacher example, too, for Mr. Hayden. The classroom teacher should model throughout this process by completing a classroom matrix and classroom mission statement. Remember that modeling is the best way to lead others. Notice how key words from each matrix are woven into the mission statements.

When they are finished, make sure they check that nothing important has been omitted. Upper-elementary and secondary students might have one or two peers read their missions and help them check for missing information. In primary grades, the teacher may need to be somewhat more directive.

Mission statements are useless unless they orient and align our activities. In working with schools and not-for-profits, I often see nonspecific missions that do little to guide schools in their continuous improvement journeys. They are filled with high-sounding phrases like "create lifelong learners" that are difficult to measure. If you can't measure it, how will you know that you are actually developing students with these attitudes and skills? That's why we never write mission statements until stakeholder needs and system goals have been identified.

A few years ago I visited a classroom in which the class mission statement was prominently displayed on an interior bulletin board. Each student (and the teacher) had signed the chart, indicating willingness to try to achieve the challenging goals. As I read this mission statement, it was evident how carefully the words had been crafted. Each sentence contained one or two challenge targets that could be easily measured. There were no ambiguous phrases. Several charts were posted beside the mission statement. I asked the teacher if one of her students would explain. A very confident student volunteered. He told me that the charts were updated each week to show how well the students were demonstrating the various aspects of the mission, and he pointed to one graph labeled "Reading Performance" and then to the mission statement, where there was a phrase about each student doing his or her best to read on or above grade level. A piece of colorful yarn linked the graph and the appropriate section of the mission statement. My student guide explained that they used a series of leveled reading books to determine reading performance and that any student could ask to be tested weekly, if he or she thought growth had occurred. The chart showed the grade-level results. Other charts aligned with each of the remaining measurable elements of the mission.

I worked with the food services leaders of several elementary, middle, and high schools. Our tasks were to set direction, bring about alignment, and establish the framework for continuous improvement. We started by identifying the food service employees' customers and what needs and expectations they had. Students, staff, and parents were the key customer and stakeholder groups. Initially, we conducted a brainstorming and affinity exercise to identify related customer expectations. Later, we verified the group's ideas by asking representative customers to provide feedback about our list. The cafeteria managers identified "variety of food," "good value for money," "nutritious food," "friendly service," "speedy service," and "clean and quiet environment" as a few of the most commonly identified needs. We discussed detailed expectations for each performance area. For example, one middle school suggested that "serve all eighth grade students in 15 minutes or less" would be a good performance standard to maintain. Once the customers and their needs had been identified, we were able to use this information to develop (quite quickly) a focused and measurable mission statement that read something like this:

> *The food service department of Anytown School District provides nutritious meals to students and staff in a clean, quiet environment. We strive to give good value for money and to provide our services in a friendly and efficient manner.*

I believe it is easy to see how each subcomponent of this mission statement derives from the customer matrix. It is also clear that each aspect is measurable. "Friendliness of service" can be measured using a questionnaire or interview schedule. "Efficiency of service" can be measured by clocking how long it takes to serve all eighth-grade students.

Table 2.5 How to create a measurable mission.

Performance indicator	Methods of measurement
GPA	Weekly quizzes, grades on assignments, 9-week grade report
Writing ability	Feedback on weekly assignments, school writing rubric score
Writing confidence	Self-assessment on rubric developed in class
Spanish-speaking ability	Weekly grades on assignments, number of vocabulary words mastered, Foreign Service Exam
Number of friends from other cultures	Frequency count
Public-speaking ability	Feedback provided by audience on rubric
Public-speaking confidence	Self-assessment on rubric developed in class
Ability to work in teams	Feedback provided by other team members on rubric

Here's how to ensure that investing the time in mission statement development proves to be beneficial. Once the mission is written, ask students to identify the specific things they said they will do. For example, review Richard's mission. The items in Table 2.5 are measurable.

Ensure that each of the attitudes and skills in Table 2.5 can be found in Richard's data folder and that he is regularly tracking his performance. Skills like "Spanish-speaking ability" can be measured using performance assessments. Writing ability should be measured using a "best practice" rubric. Attitudes can be measured using surveys (Likert-type scale) or interviews (with a standardized set of questions and a rubric). Once the measurement system is established, teach Richard how to record his performance data in his data folder or E-locker, and set clear expectations for maintenance of his information. Schedule regular meetings with Richard to review his performance, discuss opportunities for improvement, and establish improvement plans. If you follow through with measurement and discussion of performance, you can be sure that the personal mission is a living document that will guide and motivate learners.

My Personal Mission

I will come to school every day and behave myself so I can learn to read and write better because I have to get ready for fourth grade. And my math has to get better because next year I HAVE to know my adding and subtracting facts. I will not make anyone feel bad. I will turn in all my homework on time to show I can be responsible. If I can do all these things, my stakeholders will be VERY happy (including me)!

Signed,
Wanda Hamilton

My Personal Mission

I have many reasons to make the most of this year's learning opportunities. I have two more years, and then it's off to a university! In addition to maintaining a 3.5 GPA, I plan to greatly improve my ability and confidence in writing. Universities put much emphasis on this skill. Because I'm interested in international finance, I want to begin studying Spanish and become personal friends with as many people from different cultures as possible. This will broaden my horizons. I will also take every opportunity to perfect my public-speaking skills and to work in teams, since these are key skills for the workplace.

Signed,
Richard Jackson

Mr. Hayden's Mission Statement

My job is to teach each and every one of my students math computation, problem-solving, algebra, and geometry skills. This year, I also have a challenge to make sure that all students master their basic math facts. I will provide learning activities in an enjoyable and safe environment. I will also try my best to ensure that all students pass my course, not by watering down my standards but by using differentiated approaches and giving extra time for learning to some students. I will align my teaching with the state standards, not the textbook, so all students will pass the state test. Finally, I will communicate frequently with the parents of each of my students.

Signed,
Mr. Hayden

"In the language of Total Quality, a true learning organization optimizes its entire system—including processes and product—by empowering everyone, especially front-line workers—students and teachers in the case of schools—to continuously improve their work." (Bonstingl, 2001, p. 29)

When the customer matrix and mission statements have been created, place these in the data folders (and perhaps on the classroom's walls). Review and update these and all other data folder files periodically.

CORE BELIEFS

Conduct a discussion with students about how our beliefs and values ought to influence the way we talk and act. If we don't clearly identify our beliefs, inappropriate and unhelpful talk and behavior can occur. Sometimes, randomness may be appropriate. Creativity may be encouraged in a serendipitous environment. But for the most part, learners and workers in the classroom and elsewhere in the school ought to be guided by a few very powerful values, beliefs, or operating principles—whatever you decide to call them.

Return to the "Core Values and Beliefs" section in Chapter 1 for a review of the core beliefs that undergird this book and much of the continuous quality improvement philosophy.

Remember the core belief of "high expectations"? If we *believe* that some kids can't be as successful as others because they come from poor families and have not been provided the same opportunities as others, then we may *talk* less to them or *talk* in different ways to them (less-challenging vocabulary). In turn, we may *act* in an impatient manner when they don't immediately know the answers to questions, and we may *act* to withhold positive reinforcements (smiles, proximity, or opportunities). In such an environment, student learning *results* will be less than desired (Good and Brophy, 1987). Figure 2.1 indicates that when taken together, there is a link between our *beliefs* and the *results* that students produce. "A language of achievement is language that shows an internal locus of control. It encour-

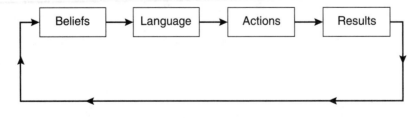

Figure 2.1 Relationship among beliefs, language, actions, and results.

ages people to openly admit and discuss mistakes while seeking to learn and develop. The result is an environment where people make fewer mistakes and rarely repeat them—a culture where people feel they have influence or control over their world. It creates a culture that openly praises and recognizes people while encouraging active problem identification and solutions" (Ray and Bronstein, 2001, p. 59).

Getting Started

In many schools, students and staff learn about programs such as Character Counts (www.charactercounts.org) to improve their performance in key areas such as behavior and academics. If you have adopted a similar approach (or strategy), start with a review of these core values in order to foster alignment with existing programs and to avoid introducing additional information into the system. Have students conduct Internet searches of "education core beliefs." Review their lists, and sort to see how frequently various concepts occur. Teach students how to do a simple "frequency count" or "checksheet" (McClanahan and Wicks, 1993) that lists the value (e.g., respect) in the left-hand column and number of times it was mentioned in the right-hand column. (see Table 2.6). Of course, just because everyone else tends to view a certain value as important doesn't mean you must. Use the results of this search and review as a starter list. Have students share their research with stakeholders to see what they think.

Next, complete a "sounds like" and "looks like" chart (Table 2.7) to help students understand exactly what it means to display or not display the core value with talk and actions. "It is much more difficult to monitor the presence of beliefs than it is to monitor the presence of behaviors. While asking the question, 'What do you believe?' could provide interesting answers that are worthy of consideration, finding shared answers to the question, 'What are you prepared *to do* in support of those beliefs?' will be much more effective in advancing school improvement" (DuFour and Eaker, 1998, pp. 96–97) (emphasis in original).

Build on students' beginning definitions, listed in the middle column of the research checksheet. Completing this activity will also help students learn the real meaning of the term or concept. These quality tools can also be used to help students learn new words in literature, social studies, or science, for example. Vocabulary development is a worthwhile goal, given the limited number of words known by the average student.

After lots of discussion and word study, and after completing the "sounds like/looks like" chart, engage in a consensogram process to select 5–10 core beliefs that will be used to govern your classroom or school as you go about the business of learning and improving. Put a chart (Table 2.8) on the overhead (without the black dots). Give students a copy to use at their seats. Explain to students about "multivoting." The multivote process gives students about one-third or one-half as many votes as there are core values. In other words, if you have 20 core values from which you want to choose a few, give each student seven (roughly one-third of 20) to 10 (half of 20) "votes" in the form of colorful sticky dots that can be purchased at office supply stores. If you don't have sticky dots, students can place a checkmark in the box when they vote.

Tell each student to independently vote for her or his most important core values. If you've given eight votes to each student, one vote can be assigned to each of eight core values, for example, or four can be assigned to "respect," two can be awarded to "success for all," and two can be used to vote for "diversity." Deciding to spend four votes for "respect" signifies that the student really believes in the importance of everyone living that core value. As long as the votes total eight, students can spend them any way they like. Table 2.8 shows how Rasheed's chart might look.

Table 2.6 Core value research checksheet: Fareeda.

Core value	What does it mean?	Frequency
Integrity	Doing the right thing, keeping my word	7
Perseverance	Sticking with something even when it gets hard	4
Teamwork	Working together to create something better than I could do alone	11
Compassion	It's like empathy or being able to feel as another person feels, especially when sad	2
Honesty	Kind of like integrity. Telling the truth.	5
Valuing Diversity	Celebrating our differences as something good	10
Leadership	Helping guide a group toward its goals. I can also lead myself in the right direction.	14

Data sources: County Economic Needs Assessment, web search of local school districts' core values lists, notes from last month's convocation, school board handbook, *Quality Journal* article, *Baldrige Education Criteria, What It Takes to Be Successful in Life,* Stephen Covey's *Principle-Centered Leadership*

Table 2.7   Sounds-like/looks-like matrix.

Core value	Sounds like	Does not sound like	Looks like	Does not look like
Respect everyone	"She is new and different, and we should make her feel welcome."	"That's a stupid idea."	When our teacher let everyone share ideas before making our decision	When those two sixth graders were calling each other bad names
Use data to make decisions	"What information helped you make this decision?"	"I guessed at the answer."	Comparing our performance with other classrooms so we'll know how we're doing	When we chose those books from the library and they were way too difficult for us to read

Each student should vote independently. Sometimes, blank charts (like Rasheed's checksheet) are hung on the wall, and students walk to the front and take turns putting their dots on the paper. But this public voting process can influence students as they begin to see how others have voted. After each student has selected her or his most important core beliefs, have students tabulate the results and create a classroom chart like Table 2.9, "Mrs. Renaldo's Classroom Core Beliefs Consensogram."

Engage students in a discussion about the results before reaching a final consensus. Place the class list of core beliefs on a "looks like/sounds like" chart that is prominently posted in the classroom.

Many people accept the importance of establishing core values or beliefs, but question how they can be used effectively. It's the "so what" question. "Core values are on my classroom wall, but I don't know how to use them effectively to positively impact my classroom or school environment." If you do the following activities, you can be sure that the core values exercise will have been worthwhile:

- Leave the core values chart up for the entire year. Make adjustments if necessary as issues arise. For example, the occurrence of a "critical incident" can lead you to discuss a new core value that students believe should be added to your list.
- Hold regular discussions about the core values, especially when you and the students have seen evidence of someone displaying a belief. It's a great way to build vocabulary and engage all students in high-level thinking such as "identifying similarities and differences" (Marzano, Pickering, and Pollock, 2001).
- Set up a charting system to track frequency of "living your core values." You can use the same consensogram chart without the dots. Now, you will be using the chart as a checksheet. Each time someone sees or hears an example of the value being demonstrated, put a dot on the chart and discuss briefly. "Percentage of students demonstrating our core values" might well be on your classroom dashboard, so it would make sense to track this important performance indicator in student and teacher data folders.
- When planning your curriculum map, design reading and writing assignments that focus on one or more of the core values. It is very easy to build thematic, interdisciplinary learning units around core values.
- Service learning and enrichment activities can be aligned to the core values list.
- Develop a simple survey (McClanahan and Wicks, 1993) that asks students and staff to comment on how well each of the values is being "lived," and use the results to guide improvement efforts.

Table 2.8   Rasheed's core beliefs checksheet.

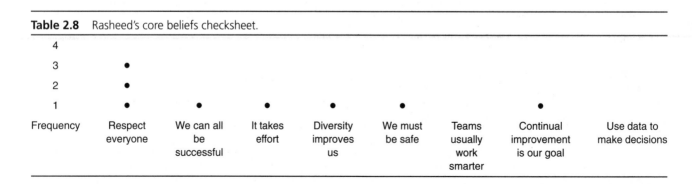

Frequency	Respect everyone	We can all be successful	It takes effort	Diversity improves us	We must be safe	Teams usually work smarter	Continual improvement is our goal	Use data to make decisions
4								
3	●							
2	●							
1	●	●	●	●	●		●	

Table 2.9 Mrs. Renaldo's classroom core beliefs consensogram.

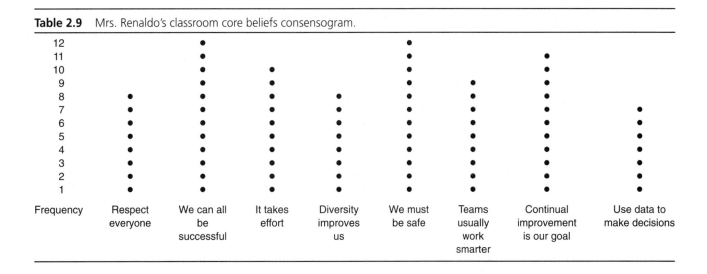

Frequency	Respect everyone	We can all be successful	It takes effort	Diversity improves us	We must be safe	Teams usually work smarter	Continual improvement is our goal	Use data to make decisions
12		•			•			
11		•			•		•	
10		•	•		•		•	
9		•	•		•	•		
8	•	•	•	•	•	•	•	
7	•	•	•	•	•	•	•	•
6	•	•	•	•	•	•	•	•
5	•	•	•	•	•	•	•	•
4	•	•	•	•	•	•	•	•
3	•	•	•	•	•	•	•	•
2	•	•	•	•	•	•	•	•
1	•	•	•	•	•	•	•	•

There are many ways to make sure that the core values are regularly discussed and implemented in your classroom and school.

Academic Standards Supported by These Activities:

- Ask questions for clarification and understanding.
- Report on a topic with facts and details, drawing from several sources of information.
- Use various reference materials, including online resources.

DASHBOARDS

I use the concept of a "dashboard" to help everyone in an organization focus on the most important performance indicators—those that tell us whether we are doing well. I help them understand the basic concept by first using a common example that we are all familiar with.

An automobile's dashboard displays such vital information as oil pressure, water temperature, RPMs, battery charge, fuel, and speed. These readings have been selected for obvious reasons—if warning lights begin flashing in any of these subsystem gauges, you may find yourself stranded (engine overheated) or reaching for your checkbook (driving too fast). So, the first useful concept that we borrow from an automobile dashboard is that of "making sure we are tracking the most important data."

When creating your dashboard, remember the importance of balance. Lawton (2002, p. 67) cautions that when developing our dashboard, we should be careful to reflect the "priorities of both the organization and its customers. To do so requires categories of measures that reflect the key values of both parties."

Lezotte and Pepperl (1999, p. 63) remind us that a focus on dashboard goals should consist of student learning indicators. "One of the important changes [required in the future] is for the system to focus on learning and the learner, rather than on teaching and the teacher. What is it, more than anything else, that we want our kids to know, do, and be disposed to do as they move through their experiences in school?" The answers should be reflected on your school, classroom, and personal dashboards. Neuman and Simmons (2000, p. 12) suggest that "good instructional practice is at the center of improving student achievement and must be aligned with an ongoing, measurable, and rigorous accountability system. This alignment is possible when all members of the education community are involved in the creation of clear expectations for performance that are tied to high academic standards for all children." Aligned and balanced school and classroom dashboards provide clear expectations of future targets for key performance indicators as well as current baseline results. Dashboards help us focus.

A second concept linked to the dashboard construct is "timeliness of data." What good would the gas gauge be if we could get an accurate reading for the amount of gas in the tank only once a year? Very little. The measures (assessments, tests, demonstrations) we select to determine student learning performance, therefore, must support frequent data generation that can be used by teachers to make instructional decisions in real time. Assessments should provide leading data that can be used to change instruction and learning experiences for the benefit of students. The ability to frequently collect performance data also allows students (some with short attention spans) to update their data folders daily, weekly, or monthly.

Your state may have an accountability test for reading, math, writing, and the state academic standards. Most everyone does. The test is probably given once a year (and sometimes only in specified grades). Such tests are designed to provide information to state and federal officials (departments of education and legislatures), but the results from this once-a-year activity cannot easily and quickly be used by teachers to improve the instruction for the students they have today. In many states, the data are returned to teachers long after the students have been sent to the next grade.

To be successful in today's accountability-driven environment, many important questions must be asked by teachers, administrators, and students. The questions include these: "How can we measure student reading ability day-to-day and week-to-week so instruction can be adjusted appropriately? How can I ensure that my students are mastering the state's academic standards as I teach them? And if they are not attaining mastery, what can I and my colleagues do?" You will need to identify and begin implementing such tools as running records and leveled books if you want to be able to include "percentage of second grade students reading on or above level" on your grade-level dashboard. Assessments such as the Developmental Reading Assessment (DRA) or Dynamic Indicators of Basic Early Literacy Skills (DIBELS) allow real-time instructional decision making. A team should research the best assessments for your grade and school (and hopefully, district) so everyone is aligned with the best practices you can find. When you have frequent, leading measures in place, data can begin to inform improvement decisions. "If data do not guide improvement efforts, schools will continue to base decisions on a mixture of intuitions, beliefs, philosophy, and hypotheses" (Heritage and Chen, 2005, p. 708).

Recently, I observed a meeting between a second-grade teacher, a reading specialist, and a principal. The purpose of this collaboration was to review the latest (monthly) reading assessment data. Things weren't going well. Many students in this particular classroom were not progressing as well as their peers in other rooms, and they were in danger of not meeting end-of-year performance targets. After a brief but very focused discussion, the decision was taken to double the time the students spent on reading each day. The classroom teacher would continue to provide the same amount of instruction for the students (although some adjustments were made to instructional practices), and the reading specialist would work with the students for an additional hour each day. Appropriate decisions can be made for the best interests of the students when teachers regularly collect "leading" data and when a spirit of continuous improvement has been nurtured.

Huggett summarizes the philosophy and techniques behind the dashboard:

> *What gets measured gets done. . . . An effective measurement system that scans both the lagging (outcome) measures and leading indicators to allow mid-course corrections can and should become the framework for managing change. Keeping track of what is being done in the name of strategy deployment (ensuring everyone is pulling in the same direction) can only be accomplished with an effective measurement system that is tied to your strategy. Since you can't make every decision yourself, your measurement system becomes one of your most critical tools for communicating what is important and should be considered at every decision point. . . . After clarifying the desired destination, the leadership team creates a "dashboard" of the critical few key indicators. . . . After the leadership team has developed its dashboard, it is presented to the next level of the organization with this message: "This is what we are watching. Design a dashboard that is appropriate for your work and that is aligned with and supports our dashboard." This process continues until each level and department in the organization has designed its own dashboard. All dashboards are linked and aligned, both vertically and horizontally and support the organization's strategy (1999, pp. 38–39).*

Ideally, the school (e.g., teachers, students, administrators, parents, and other stakeholders) will decide what should be on the dashboard, although actual indicators and measures may vary somewhat by grade level and subject area. If the school has not developed its dashboard, it is helpful when teams of teachers can agree what to include as their key performance indicators. Setting the focus areas for the performance indicators is a fairly quick and relatively painless task, especially when you use quality tools such as multivoting, affinity charting, benchmarking, and/or consensograms. All schools in the nation will have reading, writing, and math on their dashboards. But the next step—agreeing on measures—is somewhat more difficult. Rarely have most grade levels or schools engaged in collegial dialogue and research to select a set of common measurement tools that will yield reliable and valid data for decision making. Some work is usually required before a school is ready to identify, recommend, and reach consensus on agreed grade level and school measures (reading assessments, writing rubrics, math facts timed tests, etc.). A sample dashboard appears in Table 2.10.

Once performance indicators and measures have been agreed upon, you can collect baseline data and set targets. Some schools make eye-catching displays at the entrance to their buildings that approximate the examples shown in Figures 2.2 and 2.3. The charts always display aggregated school data—they never identify individual teachers and students. Solid lines indicate goals or targets and dotted lines indicate current performance. Recently, I saw several very creative examples of dashboards displayed at the entrance to schools. One chose the theme "Reaching for the Stars," and the dashboard gauges were shown in the cockpit of a spaceship. Bright colors drew me in to look at the performance data and goals posted on the charts. Of course, you are not locked in to this or any other type of display. The important criteria to be met include:

- Reflective of the five to seven most important performance indicators (with the bulk focusing on learning)
- Quick and easy for teachers and students to create and maintain
- Easy to interpret the data
- Large enough to be read from a distance
- Does not identify individual students or teachers

Table 2.10 Mr. Kwan's (grade 2) dashboard of performance indicators and measures.

Goal focus	Leading measures	Frequency	Whose data folders?
1.0 Percentage of students reading and writing on or above grade level by disaggregated groups with no significant differences in performance	1.1 Percentage on/above level as measured by DRA and leveled books	Biweekly/monthly/quarterly	Student, teacher
	1.2 Percentage mastery on language arts criterion-referenced mastery tests on state standards	Biweekly	Student, teacher
	1.3 Percentage mastery on district quarterly assessments on state standards	Quarterly	Teacher
	1.4 Percentage on/above level as measured by school writing rubric	Monthly/quarterly	Student, teacher
2.0 Percentage of students mastering state performance standards in math by disaggregated groups with no significant differences in performance	2.1 Percentage score on unit tests in math class	Weekly/biweekly	Student, teacher
	2.2 Percentage mastery on school quarterly assessments on state standards	Quarterly	Teacher
	2.3 Percentage mastery on math criterion-referenced tests on state standards	Biweekly	Student, teacher
	2.4 Percentage meeting standard on school math facts tests	Weekly	Student, teacher
3.0 Percentage attendance	3.1 Percentage of student attendance	Daily	Student, teacher
4.0 Percentage of students with appropriate/ inappropriate behavior	4.1 Percentage in each of four levels of Raise Responsibility System (Marshall and Weisner, 2004)	Daily	Student, teacher
	4.2 Percentage of office referrals	Daily	Teacher
5.0 Percentage of students with quality homework submitted on time	5.1 Percentage of students with on-time, satisfactory homework	Daily	Student, teacher

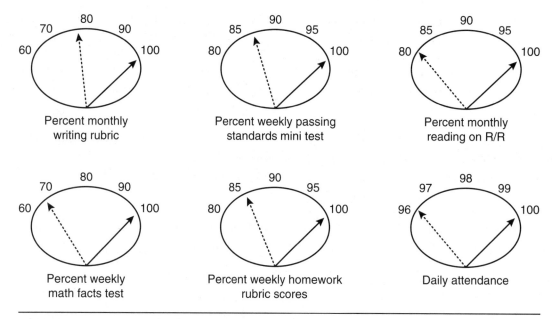

Figure 2.2   Mr. Carlson's dashboard of key performance indicators.

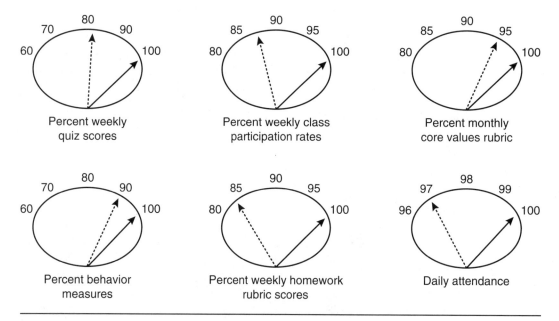

Figure 2.3   Mrs. Jenkins's dashboard of key performance indicators.

As long as you adhere to these criteria and others that your team identifies, you will maintain focus on the most important performance indicators for your classroom and school. Remember: It's not about making interesting charts to take care of that age-old problem of "What do I put on my walls?" The dashboard display should be seen as a lighthouse tool—one that helps you steer your ship in the proper direction.

STUDENT DATA FOLDERS

I know of no other tool-as-quality-philosophy that can engage students in taking responsibility for their own learning results as well as the data folder. If used properly, data folders can also engender increased and better quality communication between the school and the home.

Stiggins (2004, p. 27) suggests that improving achievement in schools, at least in part, requires "deep student involvement in day-to-day classroom assessment, record keeping, and communication. Through student involvement in classroom assessment, we can focus students on a clear path to ultimate success. If we engage students in continuous self-assessment over time, we can keep them believing that success is within reach if they keep striving. And if we provide them with the opportunity to use this evidence to tell the story of their success, such as in student-led parent/teacher conferences, we can tap a wellspring of confidence and motivation to learn that resides naturally within each student." Schooling "needs to involve students in their own education by training them to evaluate the learning process and accept responsibility for their learning" (Goldberg and Cole, 2002, p. 10).

I have seen veteran teachers, after experiencing the value of data folders in their classrooms, stand in front of dozens of colleagues and speak with enthusiasm bordering on religious conversion. Consider this quotation from Diana, a kindergarten teacher: "I have used data folders for two years, and I love it! It works. I just had five more children hit the 100 Club [able to count to 100] in the last week. They have been highlighting away [recording their progress on charts]. A different color each quarter. I have two little guys who have been pulling out their data folders every day for two weeks to practice, without me requesting them to do so. Finally, they both have made it. One at 2:45 today, six days left for this school year. So I had to run around and find a proper reward and put his name up on our success board. One beautiful little girl, one of my ENL (English as a new language) students, took a practice sheet home today. They know where the sheets are, and she just picked it up on her own and walked out the door with it. She is determined to make it to the 100 Club next week. Seventeen out of 24 are in . . . the most amazing part is the five who've made it within the last week . . . usually kids are finished by now . . . I know I am, and these little guys are still motivated . . . because of that daily visual they see!"

Diana and her kindergarten students have internalized the Theory Y (McGregor, 1960) belief that "the average person learns, under proper conditions, not only to accept responsibility but also to seek it. Avoidance of responsibility is a general consequence of experiences. It is not an inherent human characteristic" (Marshall and Weisner, 2004, p. 500). And if this is true for five- and six-year-olds, why can't all students learn to be more responsible and accountable for their own learning? The answer is, "They can!"

Students establish, maintain, and use the performance information contained in their data folders to guide continuous improvement activities and to track gradual progress toward learning targets. Data folders encourage and inspire improved learning results, because when "students graph their own progress [they] find it motivating to 'make the line go up'" (Safer and Fleischman, 2005, p. 82).

Development and continual use of data folders helps teachers, students, staff, and principals live the core values of:

- Personal responsibility for learning
- Continuous improvement
- All students can be successful
- Use data for decision making
- Focus on results

Lezotte and Pepperl (1999, p. 113) advocate the creation of a culture that "encourages students to self-monitor and to self-correct. Ultimately, that's what adult life is about—being reflective on our own behaviors and, where we see needs or wants, making plans and adjustments. We want to model this behavior first, and teach it second." Glasser (1990, p. 431) writes that students should "evaluate their classwork, homework, and tests and to put their evaluation of the quality of their work on everything they do" and then "keep their own records of the quality of what they do so that they always know exactly how far they have come." Chappuis and Stiggins (2002, p. 41) also weigh in on the importance of actively engaging students in assessing their own learning: "We tend to think of students as passive participants in assessment rather than engaged users of the information that assessment can produce. What we should be asking is, "How can students use assessment to take responsibility for and improve their own learning?"

Eisner (2002, p. 582) believes that schools should help students "gradually assume increased responsibility for framing their own goals and learning how to achieve them. We want students eventually to become the architects of their own education." Student-created and student-maintained data folders, complete with their clear specification of learning goals, action plans for achieving those goals, and regularly recorded progress, offer a good starting point. In essence, the data folder can become an individual education plan (IEP) for each student. "Student involvement means that students learn to use assessment information to manage their own learning so that they understand how they learn best, know exactly where they are in relation to the defined learning targets, and plan and take the next steps in their learning" (Chappuis and Stiggins, 2002, p. 41).

A data folder can be a physical thing (most commonly a three-ring binder in elementary and perhaps middle school) or it can be more intangible (an Excel file or e-locker at the secondary level). However you perceive of it, a data folder contains frequently recorded performance results for each student or adult. Performance data are maintained for each of the dashboard (the most important five to seven) school performance indicators. In the beginning, most schools will probably choose to track performance in reading, writing, math, attendance, behavior, homework, and mastery of the standards. Other important areas can be added, depending upon the direction the school is taking (e.g., tracking how well students "live" particular core values or how many service learning hours each student contributes). Include the customer matrix, personal mission, and core values in the data folder.

More information will be provided later about the various ways you can use the data folder (e.g., student-led conferences, S2S talks). Essentially, the data folder is intended to help all workers in the learning system maintain focus on the most important dashboard indicators and regularly review performance so that "real-time adjustments can be made to plans. That's why it's so important to have measures that can provide data on a frequent basis (daily, weekly, or monthly). Frequently sampling performance allows students, teachers, staff, parents, and administrators to redesign learning activities and daily schedules in order to provide the maximum support for each student.

Many elementary school teachers regularly require students to take their data folders home with them. At the middle and high school levels, parents may be able to view data folder results online. No matter what vehicle you provide, the important point is that responsible adults are being afforded more frequent opportunities to review student progress toward specific learning goals. And when adults have more and better information, they can become more involved in the learning process.

The data folder charts shown in Figures 2.4 through 2.9 indicate a few elements that should characterize each form, including clear targets such as end-of-year grade-level goals and interim student goals, a place for students to write their strategy steps for achieving improved performance, and the data chart. You may also choose to provide a space for student "reflection." When students record their performance data, they are expected to think about their results in comparison to short-term and end-of-year targets and to critically self-appraise effort and implementation of personal improvement plans. After reflection, students update their goals and strategies as necessary. "Goal setting requires assessment and problem-solving skills as well as application and organization. Students are active in the process, developing original thinking, lateral thoughts, personal independence, and responsibility" (Rader, 2005, p. 123).

Remember to start slowly, tracking a few simple performance indicators on your developing dashboard. Many teachers will start with attendance and behavior, tracked daily. Some choose to include homework. Once measures have been identified, gradually add learning results for reading, writing, math, and standards, as well as other key indicators.

Figure 2.9 suggests that having students track "effort" might be a good idea. Marzano, Pickering, and Pollock (2001, p. 52) advise that students need to "understand the relationship between effort and achievement. Teaching *about* effort . . . might work for some students, but others will need to see the connection between effort and achievement for themselves. A powerful way to help them make this connection is to ask students to periodically keep track of their effort and its relationship to achievement" (emphasis in original). The effort/achievement chart shown on page 39 is an example of a relationship chart (McClanahan and Wicks, 1993).

| | = Good quality | | = Not so good | | = My cow ate my homework |

My goal is to turn my homework in on time and in a quality level 3 manner everyday. I will do my homework at my desk from 6:00 to 7:00 every night. On weekends, Ill do it Frid ay night so I don't forget. I will check the classroom homework rubric to make sure my work is "good quality" every time. Signed, Tamara

Sunday	Monday	Tuesday	Wednesday	Thursday	Friday	Saturday
						1
2	3	4	5	6	7	8
9	10	11	12	13	14	15
16	17	18	19	20	21	22
23	24	25	26	27	28	29

Figure 2.4   Tamara's homework recording sheet.

Choose performance indicators and measures that allow real-time, leading data collection. Frequent monitoring, recording, and reflection (see Stiggins, 2002, for example) regarding specified performance indicators allow quick adjustments when necessary and opportunities for spontaneous celebrations. Good and Brophy (1987), in a review of research on goal setting, indicate the importance of "proximal" rather than "distal" performance appraisals tied to goal sets. Proximal means "performance on a task to be attempted here and now rather than to attainment of some ultimate goal in the distant future" (p. 313).

Academic Standards Supported by These Activities:
- Recognize cause and effect relationships.
- Interpret a graph representing a given situation.
- Use a variety of methods, such as words, numbers, symbols, charts, graphs, tables, diagrams, tools, and models to solve problems, justify arguments, and make conjectures.
- Explain which types of displays are appropriate for various sets of data.
- Represent data on a number line and in tables, including frequency tables.
- Represent, compare, and interpret data using tables, tally charts, and bar graphs.
- Plot and label whole numbers on a number line.
- Draw line segments and lines.

Behavior Key: 😊 = Good day   😐 = Not so good   😞 = Bad day

Attendance Key: P=Present T=Tardy A=Absent

My goals are to be present at school every day that I'm not sick and to have perfect behavior all year. I will cover my mouth with my sleeve when I cough. I will wash my hands lots. On days when I don't want to come to school, I'll remember my goals and how much work I have to do. I will follow the classroom rules. Signed, Tamara

Sunday	Monday	Tuesday	Wednesday	Thursday	Friday	Saturday
	Vacation	1 A	2 😊 P	3 😊 P	4 😊 P	5
6	7 😊 P	8 😊 P	9 😊 P	10 😊 P	11 😊 P	12
13	14 😊 P	15 😊 P	16 😊 P	17 😊 P	18 😊 P	19
20	21 😐 T	22 😊 P	23 😊 P	24 😊 P	25 A	26

Figure 2.5   Tamara's behavior/attendance chart.

TEACHER DATA CHARTS

In *The Performance Culture*, Ray and Bronstein (2001, p. 148) write that teams should maintain data for their goals and discuss results regularly with leadership. In schools, teachers should maintain their own data folders, tracking results for the performance indicators that have been established as part of the school's dashboard. Safer and Fleischman (2005, p. 81) write that "by regularly measuring all skills to be learned, teachers can graph changes in the number of correct words per minute (reading) or correct digits (math) and compare a student's progress to the rate of improvement needed to meet end-of-year goals." When the rate of progress is not adequate, changes in instructional or work strategies can be engineered. Teachers and principals who maintain their own data folders (aligned with the dashboard), as they expect students to do, are modeling best practices—best life practices—for students.

Teacher data folders contain confidential information that each teacher maintains, much like a diary or journal. Teacher data folder charts display individual and group performance (an average of all results, scatter plots). Aggregating the data provides a clear indicator to teachers regarding the relative performance of individual students as well as how their class results compare to others.

Occasionally, you may choose to show aggregated (class or grade level average) information to a student in a private conference for the purpose of helping an individual student understand where his or her performance is in relation to others, as well as to hoped-for end-of-year targets. This kind of feedback "draws an even bigger picture by telling students where they are now relative to the defined learning targets—and where teachers ultimately want them to be" (Chappuis and Stiggins, 2002, p. 42).

On the data chart, indicate your performance expectations for each performance indicator as well as key strategies that you will utilize with students (see Strategic Planning section, p. 40). Teachers should not spend much

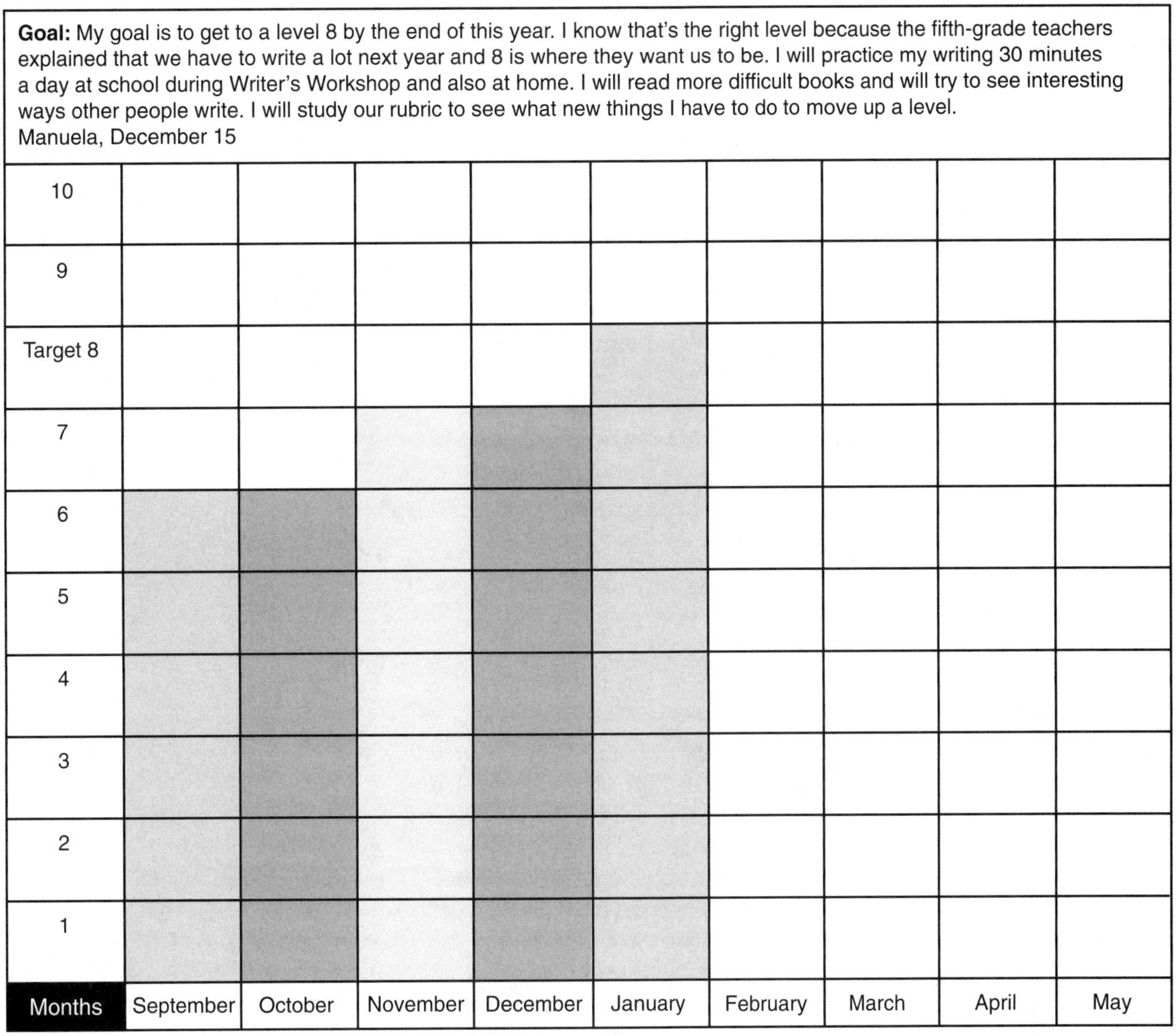

Goal: My goal is to get to a level 8 by the end of this year. I know that's the right level because the fifth-grade teachers explained that we have to write a lot next year and 8 is where they want us to be. I will practice my writing 30 minutes a day at school during Writer's Workshop and also at home. I will read more difficult books and will try to see interesting ways other people write. I will study our rubric to see what new things I have to do to move up a level.
Manuela, December 15

	September	October	November	December	January	February	March	April	May
10									
9									
Target 8					▓				
7			▓	▓	▓				
6	▓	▓	▓	▓	▓				
5	▓	▓	▓	▓	▓				
4	▓	▓	▓	▓	▓				
3	▓	▓	▓	▓	▓				
2	▓	▓	▓	▓	▓				
1	▓	▓	▓	▓	▓				
Months	September	October	November	December	January	February	March	April	May

Figure 2.6 Writing level tracking sheet: Manuela.

time preparing data folder charts. Teams can decide how they want to chart their data, and each person can take responsibility for creating paper forms that can be duplicated. You can design your data charts in any one of a dozen styles. You and your colleagues might decide to pattern your charts after the ones shown in *The Quality Rubric*, or you can draw inspiration from other quality tools books that I have referenced. Regardless of how your charts look, when you set clear performance expectations and start to track the data, students and teachers will take more responsibility, and performance will improve.

As collaborative learning groups have become more popular in schools, principals and teachers have occasionally found it difficult to maintain focus. "What should we talk about during next week's collaboration?" is an often-heard question. Review of teacher data folder performance charts in collaborative learning groups provides direction to what may otherwise deteriorate into paper grading and e-mail checking.

Once data charts have been finalized, and you have several weeks of data recorded, meet with colleagues to discuss performance compared to goals and, if necessary, to seek ideas for improvement. For example, if you've

	Week 1	Week 2	Week 3	Week 4	Week 5	Week 6	Week 7	Week 8	Week 9
Monday	67		89	88	87	88			
Tuesday		45		87					
Wednesday	79		90			83			
Thursday		78	93						
Friday	69			92	76	95			

We have at least three short quizzes each week, and I want to get no less than an 80 on each one.
Student name: _____

Reflections:

Week 1: *Well, not as good as I'd like, but I think next week will be better. The chapter looks easier.*

Week 2: *Wow! Algebra is hard. I thought I could get by with the same amount of studying that I did last year in seventh grade, but I don't think that is going to cut it. I'll have to spend more time at night on my homework. May have to ask questions in class.*

Week 3: *That's better. I put my new plan in place. Studying an extra 45 minutes at night. I've also started going to a study session with a couple of friends.*

Week 4: *On track.*

Week 5: *I didn't have time to study Thursday night. Had to go to the hospital to visit Grandma. I'll do better next week.*

Week 6: *I didn't understand an important concept following the Tuesday class, and I failed to ask the teacher for extra help. My fault.*

Figure 2.7 First quarter algebra 1 quiz scores: Jacob Watson.

set a class goal of 100 percent of homework assignments turned in on schedule and completed at a Level 4, based on the class or grade-level homework rubric, you would maintain the following charts (Figures 2.10 and 2.11) in your data folder and compare your results with those of your team members.

You may also have decided (during week 2) to briefly review the class performance for "on-time submission" and encourage all students in your class to review their personal plans regarding homework completion and submission on or before due dates. At the same time, you might compliment them on their "quality" homework performance levels and review the common faults you see in some students' work (always anonymous) in order to help all students continually improve. Following these performance talks, allow students time to review personal performance and make needed changes in the goals and strategies recorded in their data folders.

Recording information in teacher data folders and sharing this information at S2S meetings are important uses of performance data. For example, Mrs. Royce would likely share data similar to that shown in Table 2.11 with

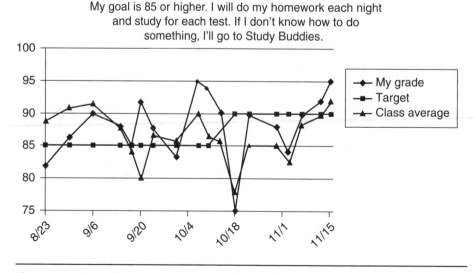

Figure 2.8 Richard's grades in Mrs. Donatello's grade 7 math class.

I know that hard work usually results in better achievement, so I'll do my best to work at a level 3 so my results will be in the A or B range. Domingo, October 12					
	F	D	C	B	A
E3. I completed the task, even though I had difficulties.				• (9/14) • (9/10)	
E2. I exerted some effort, but difficulties stopped me.		• (9/5)	• (9/7)		
E1. I exerted very little effort.	• (9/2)				

Figure 2.9   Domingo's effort/achievement chart for Mrs. Roswell's physics class.

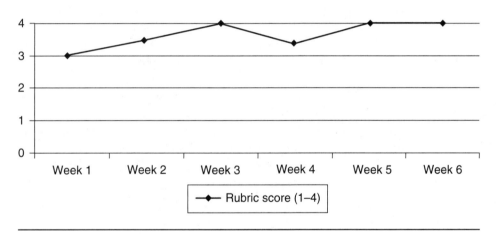

Figure 2.10   Class homework performance: Quality level 4 goal.

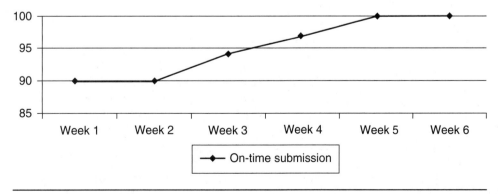

Figure 2.11   Class homework performance: 100% goal.

her principal during regular quarterly performance review meetings. During the discussion, she would explain that her class has made progress toward their reading goals and that everyone appears to be on track to meet end-of-year targets. With this knowledge, the principal can speak to the class during regular classroom walkthroughs, congratulate the students on their hard work and success, and encourage everyone to continue following their learning plans so they can reach their goals.

Tables 2.12 and 2.13 and Figures 2.12, 2.13, 2.14, 2.15, and 2.16 show sample teacher data folder charts, including one that tracks "enthusiasm for learning," a unique and "out of the box" performance indicator I learned about when visiting Community Consolidated School District 15, Palatine, Illinois recently. CCSD15 won the Baldrige award in 2003, and we went there to "benchmark" them.

Academic Standards Supported by These Activities:

- Formulate questions that can be addressed with data and collect, organize, and display relevant data to answer them.
- Apply and adapt a variety of strategies to solve problems.
- Ask questions for clarification and understanding.
- Use visual aids such as pictures and objects to present oral information.
- Recognize cause-and-effect relationships.

You can design your data charts in any one of a dozen styles. You and your students might decide to make them look like the ones shown in this section, or you can be creative and make them look like a car's dashboard. Engage students in designing charts for each of your dashboard performance indicators. When you set clear performance expectations and start to track the data, students will take more responsibility and performance will improve.

STRATEGIC PLAN DEVELOPMENT

Although the value of strategic planning in education has recently been questioned (Schmoker, 2004), no one would suggest that not having plans is a good thing. "Setting and achieving goals is one of the best ways to measure your life's progress and create unusual clarity. Consider the alternative—just drifting along aimlessly, hoping that one day good fortune will fall into your lap with little or no effort on your part" (Canfield, Hansen, and

---

Table 2.11 Mrs. Royce's class reading results.

Our goal is for everyone to read at least at a level J by May.								
N								
M								
L								
K						••		
J (class goal)					•	••••		
I				••	••••	••••		
H		•	••	••••	••••	••		
G	•	••••	••••	•••	••	•		
F	••	••••	••••	•••••	••••	•••		
E	••	••	••	••••	••••	••••		
D	••••	••••	•	••	••			
C	•••	••••	••••	•				
B	•••••	••	••••					
A	••••							
Reading level	**Sept**	**Oct**	**Nov**	**Dec**	**Jan**	**Feb**	**Mar**	**Apr**	**May**

Table 2.12 Mrs. Chavez's class writing level tracking sheet.

Goal: Everyone in my class will make progress this year in writing. The end-of-year goal is level 8, which is the expected level for promotion to the next grade. Students should practice writing 30 minutes a day during Writer's Workshop and also at home. Reading more difficult books and thinking about interesting ways other people write will help. We will regularly study our rubric to see what new things they have to do to move up a level.

	September	October	November	December	January	February	March	April	May
9									
Target 8					☺				
7			☺☺☺	☺☺☺	☺☺☺				
6		☺☺☺☺	☺☺☺	☺☺☺	☺☺☺☺				
5	☺☺☺☺	☺☺☺	☺☺☺	☺☺☺	☺☺☺☺				
4	☺☺☺☺	☺☺☺	☺☺☺☺	☺☺☺☺	☺☺☺				
3	☺☺☺	☺☺☺☺	☺☺☺	☺☺☺	☺☺				
2	☺☺☺	☺☺☺☺	☺☺	☺☺	☺				
1	☺☺☺☺								
Months	September	October	November	December	January	February	March	April	May

Hewitt, 2000, pp. 61–62). The ineffectiveness of strategic plans and goal setting activities can be attributed to problems with scope, amount of resources invested, and ultimately, what actions arise from the planning effort.

For my purposes, I simply mean the following when I refer to strategic plan development: specifying what you want to achieve (your goals), knowing what approaches you will adopt in order to achieve your goals, and setting some fairly detailed action plans to implement the approaches. Follow-on activities include checking to make sure deployment of strategies and action plans occurs and recognizing staff when actions are taken according to plan and when leading data begin to turn in the right direction.

When beginning a discussion with educators about the importance of data and strategic planning, I make this comment to stimulate thought: "Let's assume that I'm a newly elected school board member. At one of the first meetings, I ask the superintendent (Julia) for data regarding the percentage of pre-K–12 students in our learning system who read at or above grade level. I say that I'd like to see it before the next board meeting, and that I want to review recent leading data, not the state test data." When I ask the group to predict the superintendent's capability to respond, the typical answer is that Julia will probably find a few classrooms, and maybe an entire elementary school, that can provide the type of information that I'm requesting, but that she will be unable to return with the system-wide data that I seek. We then discuss how my simple question can exert powerful influence on the organization.

Table 2.13 Mr. Andrews's class: Weekly enthusiasm for learning chart.

Our goal is to work together (teacher and students) to maintain high levels of enthusiasm (100% in the top two categories each week). When we find that we aren't enthused, we'll discuss reasons why and try to make improvements.

Enthusiasm levels	Ecstatic	Moderately enthused	Disenchanted	Ecstatic	Moderately enthused	Disenchanted	Ecstatic	Moderately enthused	Disenchanted
	Week 1			Week 2			Week 3		

Number of students voting in each column

Time

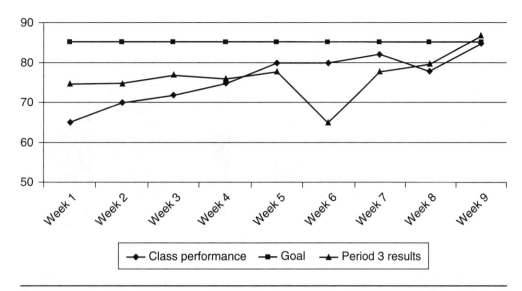

Figure 2.12 Division facts tests.

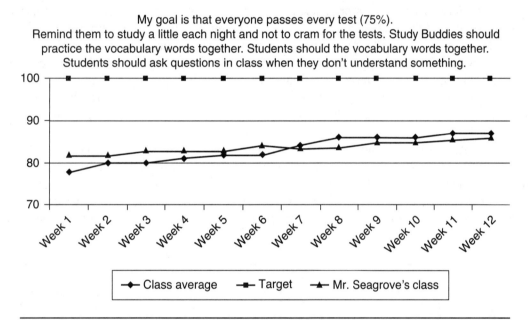

Figure 2.13 Mr. Hamza's Spanish class tests.

Let's now assume that several weeks, perhaps months, have passed, and in that interval, the system has chosen best-practice measures, trained teachers how to use the tools, and gathered the data for all K–12 students. I now have disaggregated results for all our students. To simplify, let's say that the district average rate of reading on or above grade level is 67 percent. What are the logical next questions that I will ask? I'll probably inquire, "Why do we only have two-thirds of our students reading at desired levels, and what strategies does this learning system have in place to increase the success rates?" Asking and answering these questions is at the heart of strategic planning and continuous improvement. Later, you will see how System-to-System talks help ensure that strategies are implemented and goals achieved—all through simple Socratic supervision.

Organizations spend far too much time planning and too little time implementing and learning from the implementation. In essence, we become stuck at the P phase of the PDCI cycle, forgetting that the three other steps are at least as important. But this need not be the case, once you understand about quality improvement and the role of strategic planning. "Strategic planning, if it is true to its name and origin, will result in a completely new way of

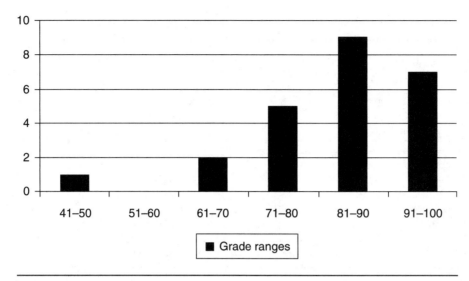

Figure 2.14 Histogram: Mr. Tyler's period 4 math results.

thinking and acting. 'Organization' transforms itself into a verb, and it involves every aspect, every energy, every intelligence of those bonded together by common values and committed to a mutual purpose" (Cook, 2004, p. 83).

Today, superintendents are the CEOs of multi-million-dollar organizations. Principals also may oversee the operation of a school whose annual budget runs to a few million dollars. And teachers are directly responsible for the learning of their students. Yet, few of these leaders have taken the time to develop a detailed, written strategic plan that incorporates SMART (see page 45) goals focused on improving student learning results, best-practice strategies, and detailed action plans. Together, these elements provide clear expectations about future organizational direction.

I believe that all leaders of learning systems—classroom, school, and district—should be able to produce a strategic plan, complete with specific learning-centered goals, for review by stakeholders, much as educators are expected to have curriculum guides. "Goals structure and prioritize the work by providing a framework on which leadership can model goal-focused behavior. Teams with clear and unambiguous goals waste less time and accomplish more than groups without clear goals" (Ray and Bronstein, 2001, p. 97). Yet, the education landscape is

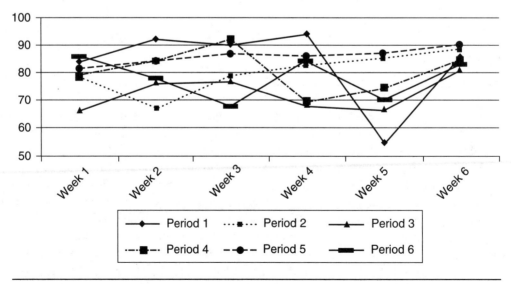

Figure 2.15 Mr. Wilson's dashboard chart 1: Percentage of homework meeting quality rubric 4/4 score.

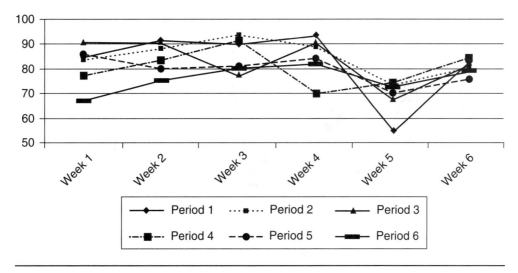

Figure 2.16 Mr. Wilson's dashboard chart 2: Percentage of students passing weekly tests.

a desert when we search for examples of good student-focused learning goals. "If we concentrate our efforts more on measurable goals, then site-based management and Total Quality Management will thrive. I do not mean that all school goals must be academic learning goals. Salient goals for processes and products are needed, too. But the last 10 years should have taught us that establishing vague process or procedural goals in the absence of clear, concrete learning goals is foolish" (Schmoker, 1996, pp. 26–27).

In a classroom, the strategic plan will begin with your dashboard indicators, SMART goals, and best-practice strategies. Canfield, Hansen, and Hewitt (2000) advise that goals should be personally crafted. They should be meaningful to you and your students. But, there should be alignment with the goals of other classrooms and with the school's dashboard. Engage students in developing their own personal and classroom goals. Goals should also be flexible, challenging and exciting, specific and measurable, realistic, balanced in scope, and in sync with your values and expressed stakeholder needs.

When you write your goals, make sure they are SMART goals. (See www.projectsmart.co.uk/smart_goals.html for additional information about SMART goals.)

Specific
Measurable
Aligned
Realistic
Time-Bound

A SMART goal reads like this: *Decrease my office referrals for bullying from last year's average of two per month to zero by the end of this school year as measured by the monthly principal's behavior report.*

Is the goal specific? Yes. Anyone reading this goal statement will understand exactly what we intend to accomplish as a class.

Is it measurable? Yes. The measure is defined as the "monthly principal's behavior report." The school may need to standardize what "bullying" means, however.

Is it aligned? Probably, but we don't know because we can't review the school's strategic plan or dashboard. We do know that many schools are working to reduce bullying, so we are fairly certain this goal will align well with the overall school direction.

Is it realistic? Well, maybe or maybe not. We do know that the average last year was two referrals per month. It would be helpful to know what the two previous years' averages were and other information such as class size (Did the student population increase from 20 to 26?), specific information about particular students (Everyone seems to get along well; no obvious problems), and strategies you will employ (Will you engage in character education and core values exercises?).

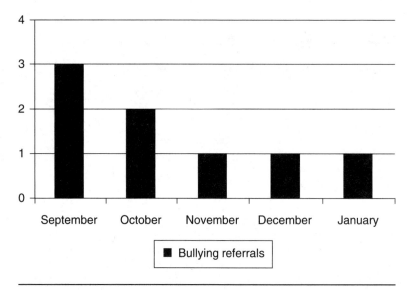

Figure 2.17   Mr. Arthur's class goal: One or fewer bullying referrals.

Is it time-bound? Yes. The goal states that you hope to accomplish the reduction by the end of the school year. Of course, if you have several months in which your bullying referrals are at one or zero, you might want to reformulate the goal and increase your performance expectation by shortening the time frame. For example, perhaps in December (Figure 2.17) before the holiday break, you might have a discussion with students; congratulate them on their success; and rewrite your class goal to state, "zero bullying referrals by March."

When reviewing the strategic plan form (Table 2.14), note that after the SMART goal has been developed, you should move to strategies. Your approaches or strategies should arise following collaborative benchmarking, research review, and root cause analysis (see page 56). For each strategy, you will need to develop specific action plans that are very detailed in terms of who, what, when, and how. All of this information, including formative or leading performance data, should be reviewed at regular System-to-System (S2S) meetings (see page 52). S2S meetings require that various levels of the learning system (student with teacher, teacher with principal, principal with superintendent) regularly meet to review key performance results and to plan for continuous improvement. You will want to take your strategic plan and dashboard interim performance data to each S2S meeting. Review of plans and performance set the agenda for each quarterly or monthly S2S meeting. System-to-System meetings should be focused on action plan and strategy deployment as well as review of interim performance results that might suggest that your strategies are working. More information about S2S meetings appears in a later section.

Work efficiently. It's desirable that a strategic plan should be developed jointly. You and your grade-level or subject-area colleagues can divide the work. Support services can collaboratively create a strategic plan that all staff within their functional areas will follow.

The sample plan shown in Table 2.14 is an example for reading—one performance indicator. Replicate this sheet for the other goal focus areas on your dashboard. Keep it simple.

STUDENT-LED CONFERENCES

In keeping with the core values of personal accountability for learning and leadership at all levels of the system, I believe that student-led conferences, reinventing the usual parent-teacher conferences, are a logical addition to your "quality repertoire."

Once student data folders have been established and data have been recorded, begin meeting with students regularly (five or six students per week, one or two per day) to have students briefly walk you through their folders. Encourage them to review class and individual goals as well as their recent performance. Discuss future changes to goals and strategies.

Table 2.14 Sample strategic plan.

Dashboard indicator	SMART goals	Best-practice strategies	Action plans
Percentage of students reading on or above grade level	Increase the percentage of students reading on grade level in my class from 67% to 90% by the end of the school year. I determined baseline performance using running records and leveled books as we agreed in this grade level.	Implement district Balanced Literacy Model.	1. Attend district summer workshop on new Balanced Literacy Model. 2. Restructure school day in cooperation with colleagues to allow extra reading and writing time. Begin new school year.
		Implement Writer's Workshop.	1. Attend district summer workshop on new Balanced Literacy Model. 2. Restructure school day in cooperation with colleagues to allow extra reading and writing time. Begin new school year.
		Increase amount of time devoted to reading and writing by 50%.	1. Restructure school day in cooperation with colleagues to allow extra reading and writing time. Begin new school year.
		With colleagues, assess comprehension monthly and regroup students among teachers for an additional 30 minutes of reading instruction daily.	1. Meet with colleagues to show them how to use running records and leveled books (summer). 2. Administer assessment jointly with each of my colleagues (first weeks of school). 3. Meet with librarian to discuss how to get more leveled books (next week). 4. Determine 30-minute time frame for working with students on basis of monthly assessment data (next collaboration time.) 5. Start regrouping four weeks into school year.

When it's time to conduct the next parent-teacher conference, talk with your principal about trying the student-led model, in which students take the lead and the teacher is in a support role. With a properly developed data folder, students will have no difficulty showing their parents what they have accomplished and what challenges remain. Don't worry. You will be sitting at the same table and can offer extra information when required. "Students achieve a deeper understanding of themselves and the material that they are attempting to learn when they describe the quality of their own work. Letters to parents, written self-reflections, and conferences with teachers and parents in which students outline the process they used to create a product allow students to share what they know and describe their progress toward the learning target. By accumulating evidence of their own improvement in growth portfolios, students can refer to specific stages in their growth and celebrate their achievement with others" (Chappuis and Stiggins, 2002, pp. 41–42).

Veteran teachers, who've probably conducted hundreds of conferences, tell me that the student-led conference is one of the best elements of quality education. Not only is it pleasing to see students taking accountability for their own performance, but also attendance at such events typically is higher because parents view their child in a

Table 2.15   Student-led conference activity list for Mrs. Dunnigan's room.

Who	What	How long
Student	Welcome and thanks. Tell parent she or he can ask questions at any time.	1 minute
Student	Read mission and core values.	3 minutes
Student	Review attendance, homework, and behavior charts.	3 minutes
Student	Review reading results.	2 minutes
Student	Review writing results.	2 minutes
Student	Review math results.	2 minutes
Student	Review academic standards results.	2 minutes
Parent	Ask questions of student and teacher.	2 minutes
Teacher	Closing comments.	2 minutes

"performing" role, much like at a musical performance or sports event. Two other benefits include less preparation before the conferences (because everything is already in the data folders) and less talking by the teacher during the conference.

Teachers who implement student-led conferences effectively are usually able to report the following outcomes:

* Students, parents, and teachers report high levels of satisfaction.
* Before the conferences, students work hard to improve their performance levels.
* Student feelings related to responsibility and accountability for their own learning increase.
* Student confidence (especially in public speaking) increases.
* Parent attendance at conferences usually increases (because their son or daughter is performing).

To make the conference run smoothly, it's a good idea to develop a process flowchart or outline to show what the students should discuss and how much time to spend on each point (Table 2.15). The teacher can model for her class how to use the flowchart (with another adult or a student acting as parent). With a little practice, students will be able to lead their own conferences, reflecting the core value of personal accountability.

Delisio (2004, pp. 1–2) discusses a few of the operational aspects of student-led conferences, writing that "during student-led conferences, teachers act as facilitators as students review their work and progress with their parents. Often students work from a portfolio filled with assignments they have collected before the conference. Some teachers also provide checklists of items for students to cover during the conference or a rough 'script' for them to follow." Checklists, flowcharts, or activities lists are important, especially the first few times your students conduct their own conferences. Remember, however, that the best flowchart will be the students' data folders. When these tools are comprehensive (aligned with the dashboard) and well organized, students can simply move from page to page within the allotted time, and they will cover all the important information that parents need to know.

Academic Standards Supported by These Activities:
* Use visual aids such as pictures and objects to present oral information.
* Report on a topic with facts and details, drawing from several sources of information.
* Support opinions with researched, documented evidence and with visual or media displays that use appropriate technology.

PROCESS FLOWCHARTS

Progress and performance occur following work. Work is scheduled using processes. Process means "a set of activities that, taken together, produce a result of value to a customer" (Hammer and Champy, 1993, p. 3). Often, if our processes are not clearly thought through, results will be poor. A "process is a system that transforms inputs into desired outputs" (Harvey, 2004, p. 43). Lalley (2001, p. 802) advises that "everything we do is a process—a series of interrelated actions—and every process can be improved. There will always be a difference between what is and what could be, and that discrepancy represents unlimited opportunities for improvement" and "armed with better methods and procedures, the same employees will invariably produce better results. If the process is right, the right results will follow."

All continuous improvement models stress the importance of processes, at least in part, because processes bring customers and suppliers together. "Each person in the school system—whether student, professional, or classified staff—is a customer, a next-in-line recipient of a product or service from others contributing to the process" (AASA, 1992, p. 11). In the beginning, the ISO 9000 quality model was largely about documenting an organization's processes, specifying owners of processes, and identifying key factors such as cycle time (the length of time required to complete the process steps) and customer satisfaction levels. The *Baldrige Education Criteria for Performance Excellence* system requires that we develop mechanisms for creating processes that add value to the organization and that we establish performance indicators for the control and improvement of each process. In education, all processes are designed to deliver improved learning results directly or indirectly (through support services such as food, transportation, health care, etc.) "The first level [of application of quality management in education] is to the management processes of a school. Sample school processes include strategic planning, recruiting and staff development, deploying resources, and alignment of what is taught, how it is taught, and how it is assessed" (Goldberg and Cole, 2002, p. 10).

Continuous improvement relies on quality tools, and many have already been discussed and demonstrated. "One of the most useful tools for analyzing operational processes is the flowchart—a simple picture of the stream of work and information" (Heiser and Schikora, 2001, p. 26). The process flowchart is a graphic display of sequential steps that lead students and adults to accomplish a much larger and more difficult task. Think of a recipe for baking a pie, for example. In the spirit of continuous improvement, process development and redesign are often the focus of quality team activities. Walton (1990, p. 109) discusses the FOCUS-PDCA process improvement method, which consists of the following steps:

Find a process to improve
Organize a team that knows the process
Clarify current knowledge of the process
Understand causes of process variation
Select the process improvements
Plan the improvement and continue data collection
Do the improvement, data collection, and analysis
Check the results and lessons learned from the team effort
Act to hold the gain and to continue to improve the process

Clearly, the core beliefs of continual improvement, teamwork, and data-driven decision making are inherent in FOCUS-PDCA. "One of the keys to life and to a healthy organization is to pursue, relentlessly, a better way. There is always a more elegant solution, a more effective process" (Cotter and Seymour, 1993, p. 6). The ISO 9000 quality system's newest iteration has gone beyond merely documenting or flowcharting processes and now requires that an organization "say what you do, do what you say, prove it, and improve it" (Anton and Anton, 2003, p. 45).

Here is how flowcharts can help you achieve higher performance levels:

1. Begin by flowcharting and documenting process steps. Often, there is no clearly identified process in place to help manage our activities. The best method of ensuring accuracy is to walk through the process yourself as you or others take notes.

2. Once the steps are put on paper, students and workers can gradually learn to use the job aid (flowchart) to help improve consistency of performance.

3. In formal audits, quality control specialists (in the case of a school, teachers may serve this role) observe to make sure the procedures are being followed as stated on paper.

4. Occasionally, someone will find a way to shorten the cycle time of a process or otherwise make the procedure more effective. The flowchart can be redesigned and improved, and the new approach holds sway until a new opportunity for improvement arises.

Let's go into a bit more detail about flowcharts. Although there are many specific rules for development of process maps or flowcharts, I agree with Heiser and Schikora (2001), who advocate beginning simply, with boxes (process steps) and diamonds (decision points). The point with development of flowcharts is to guide students, teachers, and administrators in the proper methods and, at times, to help evaluate current activities with an aim toward making improvements in the workflow. During improvement work, the team agrees to document the steps currently being followed in order to spot places where enhancements can be made.

Although the example in Table 2.16, in which there are no decision points, is not a traditional flowchart because there are no boxes, circles, diamonds, or arrows, it serves the same purpose and may be easier for some students to follow when the tasks are sequential.

In Table 2.16, development of the flowchart also serves another important purpose—that of providing students with clear expectations about work requirements. It's only fair that students know clearly what is expected before we ask them to perform. Providing clear expectations is a key learning principle that must become part of each classroom's standard operating procedures. In a sense, the Classroom and School Quality Rubrics are modified examples of flowcharts, too. Each guides you through a series of tasks toward a desired result.

In most cases, students should be involved in developing the flowchart. They will more likely adhere to the steps if they've had a hand in establishing them. The process flowchart becomes their "steps for success," not the teacher's. Often, a good technique is to have someone demonstrate the current process (already in use) or one that makes most sense (if you are designing a new process). Document each step as it is activated. When you've mapped the entire workflow, give the process map to an uninitiated person and see whether the process can be understood and followed and whether the results are satisfactory.

Another simple example could be a snack-break flowchart (Figure 2.18). When students have helped develop the rules—the steps within the process—they are much more likely to understand the reasons for the steps and to adhere to them. "Involve me, and I'm more likely to support you. Don't involve me, and I'm likely to ignore or resist you." Teachers are unhappy when the principal makes a decision without consulting them. Principals grouse when the superintendent sets meeting dates without consulting them. It's human nature. Remember this basic principle of involvement in order to make things run much more smoothly.

Daily snack-break performance can be charted on a time-run chart when results are not meeting the target (Figure 2.19). If an opportunity for improvement exists, the PDCI cycle should be implemented in order to bring behavior back in line with expectations.

Table 2.16   How to write a good research paper.

Step 1	Clearly identify the topic by stating the research questions that will guide your inquiry.
Step 2	Conduct research within the framework of questions.
Step 3	Adjust questions based on beginning learning.
Step 4	Web or fishbone the ideas into main topics that will be developed in your paper. For example, one lateral bone of the fish might hold the main idea of the first paragraph of your paper's body along with lots of supporting details.
Step 5	Check your work with peer editors and with the teacher. If necessary, go back and refine ideas.
Step 6	Write first draft of the entire paper.
Step 7	Read and edit.
Step 8	Give draft to peer editor to read and mark.
Step 9	Review comments and make necessary adjustments. Pay careful attention to grammar and mechanics at this stage.
Step 10	Publish final draft and submit to teacher.

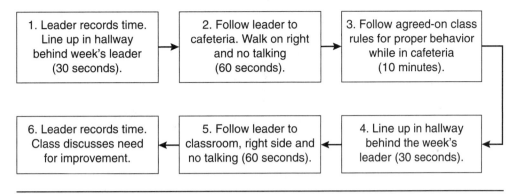

Figure 2.18   Snack-break flowchart.

A more traditional flowchart might resemble the one shown in Figure 2.20. This one has most of the bells and whistles and follows fairly standard flowcharting rules and language.

Academic flowcharts can be helpful, too. For example, you can place the steps of your writing process on the wall and in student data folders. Subtasks required for solving a complex math problem might be temporarily posted on the wall for students to check as they start their homework. You can flowchart the strategies that students should use when they encounter a difficult word or passage in their reading. Students who have trouble completing their homework at night may benefit from a "completing my homework" flowchart. Flowcharts enable students, and as a result, they become more self-reliant. Flowcharts also help systematize activities, and over time, the "best" approach can be identified for everyone to use. Confusion is reduced, and success is increased.

> *"Results tell us which processes are most effective and to what extent and where processes need reexamining and adjusting. Processes exist for results—and results should inform processes."* (Schmoker, 1996, p. 4)

Once flowcharts are developed, display them prominently in your classroom and school. The most important ones should also be placed in student data folders.

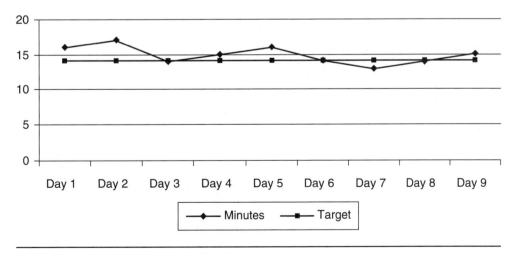

Figure 2.19   Time needed to return from break.

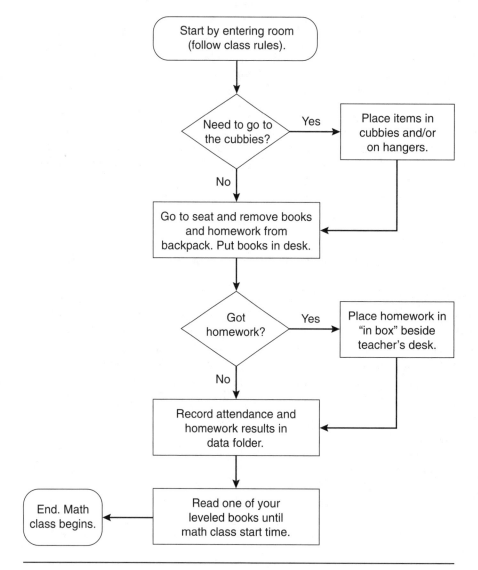

Figure 2.20   Flowchart governing first 10 minutes of class.

Note: This process chart was first developed by Mrs. Hazinga's class September 12. Updated November 23.

Academic Standards Supported by These Activities:

- Ask questions for clarification and understanding.
- Use visual aids such as pictures and objects to present oral information.
- Support solutions with evidence in both verbal and symbolic work.
- Use tools such as objects or drawings to model problems.
- Explain the reasoning used and justify the procedures selected in solving a problem.

SYSTEM-TO-SYSTEM (S2S) PROCESS

The act of collecting data is useless if we don't use the information for continuous improvement. Here are some other statements that are often true: If we think no one will check on us, we sometimes do not follow the new and better approaches (those which we've just learned). We revert to old habits. We can also slip into a habit of not measuring performance. We just work, work, work, not taking time to plan, check, and improve. And if we don't measure performance frequently, we can't make improvements to curriculum, instruction, or assessment—three critically important educational domains. In an environment where we are not driven by data to make continual improvements, student learning suffers.

I've already told you that I drive a lot. A few years ago, I traveled one stretch of road very frequently; one day, I was stopped by a trooper for speeding—just a little—and received a warning. I became more aware of that trooper and began to see him almost daily—always at different locations and times, but I could almost guarantee a sighting during the morning and evening commutes. Frequently, he'd have someone stopped alongside the highway, his patrol car's red and blue lights flashing. Where am I going with this story? Because I knew that this very persistent public servant was regularly checking my performance, my behavior changed. I made sure to put my car on cruise (strategy), setting the upper limit at the posted speed limit (desired results). That way, I knew my performance would be within acceptable levels.

System-to-System (S2S) talks are designed to ensure that we regularly check (1) implementation of key strategies and action steps and (2) interim performance for our key dashboard performance indicators. In essence, we are checking deployment of our strategic plans. S2S talks provide a systematic process to ensure that two levels of the system are reviewing and discussing the performance data—for the purpose of continual improvement. The S2S process provides required leadership, discipline, and focus in systems where drift is occurring. The kind of drift documented by Kaplan and Norton (2005, p. 76): "Our research suggests that 85% of executive leadership teams spend less than one hour per month discussing their unit's strategy, with 50% spending no time at all. Companies that manage strategy well behave differently. Top managers usually meet once a month for four to eight hours. This meeting provides the opportunity to review performance and to make adjustments to the strategy and its execution." In many schools and districts, the same is true. Superintendents do not find the time to meet regularly with building leadership to review strategy deployment and leading performance data. Bossidy and Charan (2002, p. 6) charge that leaders place "too much emphasis on what some call high-level strategy, on intellectualizing and philosophizing, and not enough on implementation. . . . Execution is not just tactics—it is a discipline and a system. It has to be built into a company's strategy, its goals, and its culture. And the leader of the organization must be deeply engaged in it."

Bossidy and Charan are talking about leaders such as Will, a superintendent, who has been reinvented by S2S talks. Will is one of the best I've seen at making and keeping commitments to be in each building monthly for two-hour S2S talks with the leadership teams. He's there asking about strategy deployment, leading performance data, and future plans for improvement. Will offers encouragement when needed, celebrates successes when goals are met, teaches when gaps in his staff's learning are spotted, and gently (usually) chides reluctant individuals forward. S2S talks are about executing the strategy. "Execution is a systematic process of rigorously discussing hows and whats, questioning, tenaciously following through, and ensuring accountability" (Bossidy and Charan, 2002, p. 22).

The education learning system in which you work consists of many levels, but the most important ones appear in Figure 2.21.

System-to-System talks require two system levels to meet and review performance data (for dashboard indicators). For example, teachers can implement a process that requires a daily S2S meeting with one or two students (individually). Students can bring their data folders, and part or all of the data can be reviewed. Teachers can reinforce positive performance and/or attempt to redirect students who are not meeting performance targets and who are probably not following their action steps.

Principals can implement S2S meetings with teachers, either individually or with grade-level or subject-area groups. Quarterly meetings can be scheduled at the beginning of each school year. The meetings should last about one or two hours. And of course, the agenda is simply a review of dashboard performance data, along with strategy and action plan implementation results. Teachers lead the meetings. The principal listens, congratulates, asks probing questions when performance has not reached desired levels, offers to provide assistance when required, and models the core values of personal accountability for learning, continuous improvement, data-driven decision making, results focus, and leadership. S2S meetings should also be conducted with support staff.

During grade-level and building-level S2S meetings, the principal acquires data to populate his/her own data folder, and this information can then be shared with the superintendent. One performance area to be included in the principal's data folder is the number of S2S meetings that have been conducted, as well as the number of classrooms that have been certified at Quality Levels 1–4, which is a key objective of *The Quality Rubric.*

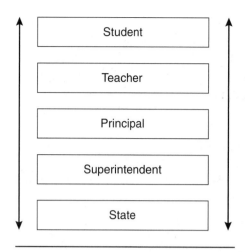

Figure 2.21 Relationship among various levels of the learning system.

Superintendents should conduct regular S2S meetings with each building principal or leadership team. In one district where the superintendent initiated monthly S2S meetings with each of his six building leadership teams, the teams report greater satisfaction. They indicate that "the superintendent is regularly in our building, and we can show him the good work we are doing." The superintendent is happier, too. He indicates that "S2S meetings have made me more of an instructional leader and changed for the better how I view my role." In this district, performance is on the rise (Figure 2.22).

Essentially, I designed the S2S Process to fill an expectation set forth in the *Baldrige Education Criteria for Performance Excellence*. The expectation is modeled by questions like these:

- How do senior leaders create an environment for performance improvement, accomplishment of strategic objectives, innovation, and organizational agility?
- How do senior leaders encourage frank, two-way communication throughout the organization?
- How do senior leaders take an active role in faculty and staff reward and recognition to reinforce high performance?
- How do you select, collect, align, and integrate data and information, including evidence of student learning, for tracking daily operations and for tracking overall organizational performance, including progress relative to strategic objectives and action plans?
- How do you review organizational performance and capabilities? How do senior leaders participate in these reviews?
- How do you translate organizational performance review findings into priorities for continuous and breakthrough improvement and into opportunities for innovations?
- How are these priorities and opportunities deployed to faculty and staff throughout your organization to enable effective support for their decision making?

In many organizations, there quite simply is no formal process to ensure that aligned goals, strategies, and action plans are in place and that regular checking of deployment of plans occurs. If these prerequisites do not exist in your organization, there can be no expectation of sustained performance improvement. That is why the System-to-System Process was developed—to bring the various levels of the system together, focused on results. The dialogue that occurs in these meetings is data-driven and direct. "You cannot have an execution culture without robust dialogue— one that brings reality to the surface through openness, candor, and informality" (Bossidy and Charan, 2002, p. 102).

A plan sheet can be created (Table 2.17) to show how principal/grade level S2S meetings can be made most effective.

A process similar to the one in Table 2.15 (although less detailed) will be used to conduct S2S talks in the classroom. Teachers are essentially engaging in S2S meetings when they sit for 5–10 minutes with individual students to review data folders. Student-led parent conferences can be thought of as another form of S2S meeting.

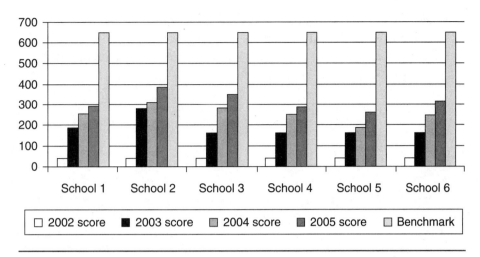

Figure 2.22   Growth in quality score.

Champy (1995, p. 74) notes that "people claim that significant change requires commitment from the top. True, the top is necessary, but it's not enough. No CEO can do this alone. You need to have a critical mass of people in the company at both upper and middle levels who are really committed to making change happen and are in it for the long haul. That critical mass has to be consistent in their actions; they all have to be speaking the same language." Although Champy is writing about business, we can draw parallels for education from his statement.

As we work to improve education, superintendents and principals are necessary ingredients. They can help or hinder improvement in student learning. But the central focus must remain the classroom—the nexus for students and teachers. When Champy talks about the "middle level," I think of the classroom teacher. You are the critically important level of the system that can make real learning improvement happen. System-to-System talks place you in a leadership role. You are clear about your goals. You and your grade-level colleagues, and other teachers

Table 2.17   Teacher/principal S2S talks plan sheet.

Task	Person responsible	Action notes (taken during meetings)
Before Meeting		
Establish the quarterly dates for S2S meetings.	Principal and grade-level leader	
Develop and improve rubrics for strategy deployment.	Teachers	
Remind participants about meeting (one week prior).	Principal and grade-level leader	
Prepare completed Strategy/Action Deployment Checksheet.	Teachers	
Prepare interim (leading) performance results for each dashboard indicator.	Teachers	
During S2S Meeting		
Present data from Strategy/Action Deployment Checksheet.	Teachers	
Discuss results and make plans for continued improvement.	Teachers and principal	
Present interim (leading) performance results for each dashboard indicator.	Teachers	
Discuss results and make plans for continued improvement.	Teachers and principal	
Summarize most important findings and action steps.	Teachers	
After S2S Meeting		
Use notes (collected in right column) to write minutes.	Grade level leader and colleagues	
Continue implementing existing and revised plans.	Teachers and principal	
Prepare for next S2S meeting.	Teachers and principal	

throughout the school, are aligned, and you use the common vocabulary that has been engendered as a result of your dashboard and strategic planning activities. Your actions are further channeled because you have selected a common set of beliefs and best practices, and you are empowered by the core values of accountability, data-driven decision making, teamwork, and continuous improvement.

QUALITY TOOLS

A number of excellent quality tools books have been written for educators. *Future Force* (McClanahan and Wicks, 1993), *Thinking Tools for Kids* (Cleary and Duncan, 1999), and *There Is Another Way!* (Byrnes and Baxter, 2005) are three of the best known. *The Quality Rubric* is not designed to provide wide-ranging and multileveled detail about quality tools. Instead, refer to the many books and journals already dedicated to this topic in order to become expert carpenters, able to pull just the right implements from the box to meet the situation's needs.

I want you to know that there is a larger framework or systems model, *within which* quality tools have a very important place, but that they are only one subsystem. I have previously discussed an important shortcoming observed in many districts and schools where much effort and many resources have been expended in support of quality tools training. *The problem is that leaders have not established support systems that will ensure systematic deployment of the tools once the training has been completed. Support systems include clear expectations for deployment, ongoing coaching, a measurement tool (Classroom and School Quality Rubrics), and recognition. That is why* The Quality Rubric *has been written.*

Just as you must be able to identify your customers and their needs, set clear goals and performance expectations, meet regularly to review performance, and engage in team-based improvement activities when there is a need or opportunity for improvement, education professionals must also be able to use a variety of structured data-gathering and decision-making tools. A number of key tools such as consensograms, checksheets, and flowcharts have already been demonstrated in earlier sections of *The Quality Rubric*.

In the following three subsections, I show how teachers, students, and principals can use a few selected quality tools to gather data and improve performance.

Teacher Example

Teachers can make great use of a fishbone diagram as an aid to problem solving. The fishbone quality tool is also known as a cause and effect chart (Walton, 1990; Cleary and Duncan, 1999). Similar tools are referred to as the five-why technique (Boukendour and Brissaud, 2005) and gap analysis. Collectively, these tools may be referred to as root cause analysis.

Root cause analysis "is a tool designed to help identify not only *what* and *how* an event occurred, but also *why* it happened. Only when investigators are able to determine why an event or failure occurred will they be able to specify workable corrective measures that prevent future events of the type observed. Understanding why an event occurred is the key to developing effective recommendations" (emphasis in the original) (Rooney and Heuvel, 2004, p. 45).

Rooney and Heuvel write that root cause analysis activity generally is a four-step process that includes data collection, causal factor charting, root cause identification, and recommendation generation and implementation. The idea is to find what caused problems and to fix them. Boukendour and Brissaud (2005, p. 26) write that the five-why technique "helps to drill deeper into the symptoms of the problem until the root cause is identified. The process starts with the statement of the problem and continues forward while asking 'Why?' whenever a cause is identified. After the question has been asked five times, the root cause usually has been discovered."

Go back in time with me a few years. I was an elementary school principal, and as such I often needed to counsel students about their behavior. I remember being called back to the office one day to talk with—let's call him Tim—one of my "frequent fliers." I asked Tim why he was at the office and not in his classroom learning. Tim said, "Because Mrs. Donaldson told me to go to the office." I smiled and asked, "Why did she tell you to go to the office?" Tim was slow to respond, but finally indicated, "Because Donna (another student) shoved me." I wondered aloud, "And why did she push you?" Tim, having been to see me on several previous occasions, was thoughtful. He cocked his head and said, "You're going to play that five-why game with me, aren't you?" I smiled and said, "Yes. So why don't you just save us some time and tell me the real reason you were sent here." "Okay," Tim agreed. "I called Donna a bad name, and that's the root cause of why I'm here." At that point, I knew we were succeeding with some of our kids in some of our classrooms. Tim (and many of his friends) were learning quality tools that could empower them and help them be more in control and, ultimately, more successful.

Here's another example of the use of "five-why thinking" from one of our schools: In a primary classroom, students had set reading goals for themselves with full awareness of their current reading levels and end-of-year expectations. At the end of the first quarter, the teacher, with accompanying student analysis, noted that many students were not making expected progress. A group meeting was held to discuss possible causes of the problem. The teacher led the students in discussing various causes and captured their thinking in Figure 2.23.

The chart shows only one or two levels of asking "Why," and you may need to delve deeper with your students. For example, when someone says, "I forget to read my book at home" you may respond with "Why do you think you forget?" If the student says, "Because I watch too much television," ask "Why do you watch too much television?" Continue until you get to a level of detail that can be translated into a possible solution for the problem. In the above example, the student might reveal that he is alone at home between 4:00 and 7:00 in the evening, and no one tells him *not* to watch TV. At that point, you can begin to suggest a process that can be implemented during the three hours when he is unsupervised. Some problems may be deeply rooted, requiring as many as five why levels of questioning.

Once a number of good causes have been identified by you and the students, discuss which ones seem most important to tackle when fixing the problem. Tell the students to think, "We want to get better at reading. If we could only select one problem to fix, what would it be?" When the most important cause has been identified, ask the same question again: "If we could select one more problem to fix, what would it be?" Continue through the top three or four contributors to poor performance.

At this stage, students can work as a group to recommend solutions to group problems ("Let's talk to the librarian about putting labels on books so we can figure out the reading levels.") They can also think about what specific things each should do to increase personal reading performance ("I should not turn on the TV until I've read for 30 minutes.")

The top group selections can be put into a Pareto chart like the one in Figure 2.24. Pareto charting reflects 80/20 thinking where "we must constantly ask ourselves what is the 20 percent that is leading to 80 percent? We

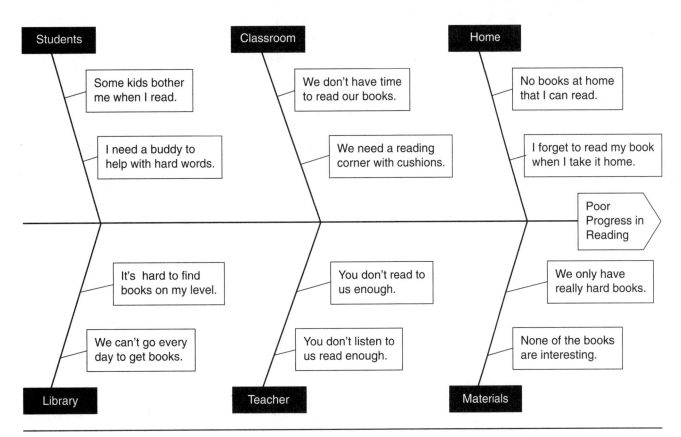

Figure 2.23 Fishbone diagram: Why second-grade students in Mrs. Johnson's class are not making progress.

must never assume that we automatically know what the answer is but take some time to think creatively about it. What are the vital few inputs or causes, as opposed to the trivial many?" (Koch, 1998, p. 38).

> *"The combination of three concepts constitutes the foundation for results: meaningful teamwork; clear, measurable goals; and the regular collection and analysis of performance data." (Schmoker, 1996, p. 2)*

The Pareto chart is typically thought of as a visual for displaying the relative share of the whole, attributed to each of several causal factors. "A Pareto chart is a series of vertical bars lined up in a descending order—from high to low—to reflect frequency, importance, or impact. Because of the descending order, Pareto charts quickly draw everyone's attention to the most important factor—providing an at-a-glace snapshot of priorities" (McClanahan and Wicks, 1993, p. 106).

In other words, when trying to solve a problem, you will identify a number of contributing causes. Life would probably be simpler if there were only one cause for every problem, but there is never only one. Once several contributing issues have been singled out, engage in discussion about which is the most important cause, which is second most important, and so on. Sometimes, this is quite easy to do, and you can place a numerical value on each cause—a weighting to indicate relative importance. Weightings (percent of total cause) are shown in the Pareto chart in Figure 2.26. The percents shown above the three bars total only 95 percent in this example, reflecting the fact that there are other minor causes that have not yet been identified.

With this information in hand, students and teachers know where to target their improvement activities. Logically, if all things are equal, you'd tackle the most important causal factor first, since by working to remove that single cause, perhaps as much as 40 percent to 60 percent of the whole problem can be eliminated. Then, you can move on to the next cause. Sometimes you might decide to tackle both simultaneously. Then, by working on the first two causes, you might expect an improvement of 60 percent to 80 percent in performance. It's Koch's idea again—focusing on the vital few that will deliver the greatest return on your investment of resources.

Once a Pareto chart has been constructed and you have a clear understanding of contributing root causes, possible solutions may now be apparent. It will be helpful to conduct an impact analysis (Table 2.18) in order to de-

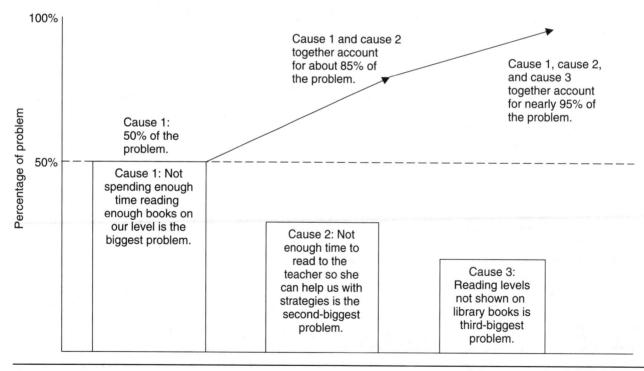

Figure 2.24   Pareto chart of most important causes of the reading problem in Mrs. Johnson's class.

Table 2.18   Impact Matrix of possible solutions for reading problems in Mrs. Johnson's class.

Very difficult		Ensure that the library purchases new, interesting books.	Get donations of leveled books so students can have books at home.
Somewhat difficult	Stop students from bothering others when they read.		Adjust schedules to allow more time for teacher to read to/with students.
Easy to implement	Assign reading buddies. Acquire cushions for reading corners.		Ask librarian to "level" all the books.
	Low impact	**Moderate impact**	**High impact**

termine which solutions will generate the best results or impact with the least disruption, effort, or resources. Table 2.18 shows a sample impact analysis matrix with two dimensions—impact or effectiveness and degree of implementation difficulty. This example is related to the previous fishbone and Pareto charts. Ideally, you will search for highly effective solutions that are easiest to implement.

If possible, Mrs. Johnson and her students will first approach the librarian about leveling all the books in the library because this is the solution with highest impact potential, and it is fairly easy to implement. Secondly, she will likely attempt to adjust her schedule to create more time when she can read with her students.

Student Example

Of course, individual students can certainly use the previous tools (brainstorming and affinity exercise, benchmarking, surveys, fishbone, Pareto charts, and impact analysis) in much the same way as the teacher examples. Time-run charts (the kind you see in data folders) are useful quality tools for students. Daily and weekly charting of results can be a powerful motivator.

The fishbone diagram can be used to help identify individual performance problems, and this graphic organizer can assist students as they group and make sense of information. The fishbone can be a great way to organize thoughts when summarizing the key points and supporting details from a social studies or science lesson, for example.

You might want to try a plus/delta exercise (Table 2.19) as an aid to student reflection and inquiry. *Plus* refers to "What worked well?" and *delta* means "What can be improved?" At the end of each week, students can be given the task of reflecting on the past five days and writing their thoughts on a plus/delta form. Start the activity by asking students to review last week's plus/delta sheet.

An expanded version of the plus/delta is de Bono's (1985) PMI activity, in which students are led to consider an idea, issue, or proposal. Systematically, they learn to consider the Plus points (good or desirable), the Minus points (bad or undesirable implications), and Interesting points (neither good nor bad at first glance but which might bear further investigation).

Table 2.19   Plus/delta form: Edward (10th-grade student).

	+	Δ
Observation number 1	**Outcome:** I got all my homework turned in on time this week and it was at least 3 or 4 on the rubric. **Why?** Because I did my homework first (before TV) like my teacher, mom, and I agreed. **Future plans:** I really need to keep on track and not forget to do it first.	**Outcome:** I did not do well on my midterm exam in English literature. **Why?** I guess I didn't read all the material that well. Especially in the beginning of the term when I wasn't so interested. **Future plans:** I have to *not* fall behind in my reading, even when it's not terribly interesting. Also, I should take good notes about what I read.
Observation number 2	**Outcome:** I joined the rugby team. **Why?** I've always wanted to play rugby, and I think it will help my self-confidence. **Future plans:** If I find that I can juggle the sports and academics, I may join another club—maybe Photography.	**Outcome:** Robert and I are still angry at one another. **Why?** I've not taken the opportunity to ask the guidance counselor to arrange a meeting so we can talk (with her help). I guess I'm a little anxious about it. **Future plans:** I'll speak to her first thing Monday morning and see if we can meet soon.

An additional implement for your beginning tool box might be a driving and restraining forces chart (Byrnes and Baxter, 2005). This idea, which has been around a long time, was originally a part of Lewin's change management model that consisted of three phases: unfreezing the current situation, making the change, and refreezing the new reality. This type of chart can be used for many purposes. For example, you might ask your middle school science students to consider a key research question such as, "What evidence can you find to support or debunk global warming?" (Admittedly, there might not be many "opposing" forces in this example, but you get the idea.) Or you could ask students to complete a force field analysis chart like the one in Table 2.20 to show what might help and hinder them from achieving their goals. This chart could then be a useful planning tool that can be included in data folders.

If you really want to introduce more levels of sophistication, you might engage the students in debating which forces are most powerful (like the Pareto/80–20 idea) and then deciding how to strengthen some while reducing others.

Other quality tools that you might teach students to use include the "issue bin" and classroom or group quality meetings. Issue bins are simply cardboard or plastic boxes in which students can drop issues that they are concerned about. Issues can pinpoint "things that should be considered for improvement," such as:

- Too much homework
- Bullying
- How to start the day more smoothly
- Cleanliness of the restrooms

Whereas other issues or suggestions might be positive or recognition issues that a student might want to bring up:

- Thanking the cooks for adding more choices to the menu
- Celebrating the hard work my classmates have done
- Complimenting the teacher on making learning fun

The items in the issue bin can be the focus for regular class continuous improvement or quality meetings. The teacher and students can vote on which ones should be discussed first, and ground rules can be laid for "dealing with the issue" and following up to make sure recommendations become part of the new fabric of classroom life. When conducting group meetings, remember to:

- Have clear objectives that are explained in an agenda so people can be thinking about them ahead of time.
- Indicate who is in charge.
- Specify rules governing talking and listening requirements.
- Set standards for positive interaction with others.
- Put students mostly in charge of the meetings.
- Assign two recorders who will take notes and write the minutes collaboratively.
- Have a follow-up mechanism to make sure actions are implemented.

Table 2.20   Force field analysis (FFA) chart.

Drivers and Restrainers for My Goal of Improving Writing Performance
Rada, November 15

Weight (1–5)	Drivers	Restrainers	Weight (1–5)
3	I practice writing 30 minutes each day.	I don't take feedback very well.	5
2	I keep a portfolio that shows how I've progressed.	I think I have "a style," and I want to develop my own approaches.	3
2	I attended a writing workshop at the public library.	I don't really like to write that much, but maybe it's because I don't think I'm good at writing.	5
1	I read a couple of books each month.	My vocabulary is pretty limited, based on a test I took.	3

Based on this FFA chart, I think I need to write and read more, and when I don't know words, I need to get the dictionary out. Also, it's pretty clear to me that I need to be more accepting of feedback and actually try to incorporate (new word—ha, ha) the comments of my teachers and peer editors into my work.

Table 2.21 Gantt chart: Ms. Brody's class preparing for student-led parent-teacher conferences.

Task	Mar 1–3	Mar 4–5	Mar 8–9	Mar 11–16	Mar 17	Mar 18
1. Take any final tests we need in order to update our data folders.	■	■	■	■		
2. Clean data folders. Make sure all pages are up to date.	■			■		
3. Develop class letter to remind parents to come on March 17.		■				
4. Develop class flowchart of what we are to say and do on March 17.			■			
5. Practice sharing our data with the teacher and Mrs. David.				■		
6. Lead my own conference!					■	
7. Write thank-you letters to parents and family members.						■

As companion to the continuous improvement process, teachers should schedule regular team meetings in which students learn to take charge of improvement activities in the classroom. The goal is for the teacher to initially model how the meetings should run, but then to gradually step into the shadows, allowing students the authority and responsibility for managing improvement.

Many teachers, reading this suggestion for the first time, will be fearful of "chaos theory" in action, and they will remember scenes from *Jurassic Park,* in which a neat little experiment went disastrously wrong. Student-run class meetings don't have to result in pandemonium. Set clear boundaries and guidelines and require students to operate well within those limits. "Boundaries are the key to empowerment. Well-defined boundaries allow people to learn how to function effectively without the danger of major mistakes" and as people "learn how to function within a set of boundaries, the boundaries should be widened to offer more autonomy and self-direction" (Ray and Bronstein, 2001, p. 127).

If you want to develop students who are responsible, trustworthy, and able to solve real problems, you have to train them how, step back, let them make a few mistakes, and redirect when necessary. "Educators are going to have to change from telling the learners what to do and how to do it, toward becoming a partner in learning with the student" (Lezotte and Pepperl, 1999, p. 34). Classroom or team quality meetings pull students together around important issues. A "combination of teamwork techniques and cooperative learning concepts can be adopted successfully to facilitate student learning" and continuous improvement (Mehra and Rhee, 1999, p. 24).

After productive team meetings, a Gantt chart might help you ensure that actions are implemented according to a specified timeline (Table 2.21). Henry L. Gantt developed these production control charts in the early part of the 20th century. You can use Microsoft Project or Excel to develop Gantt charts, or you can draw them freehand. There need not be anything fancy about quality improvement in schools. It's the thinking and the work that matter, not the beauty of your charts.

Principal Example

Recently, the leadership at Anytown High School decided to establish a school dashboard in order to set direction for the entire school community. Barry, the principal, led an exercise in which all employees and students, along with representative samples from other stakeholder groups (e.g., parents, community members), identified the most desirable performance indicators for the school's dashboard. Barry decided that "nested affinity exercises" would work best in this application. Affinity exercises can be used to sort ideas. "Sometimes you need to make ideas clear so you can think about them. Sorting them and seeing what they have in common is one way to do

> **Academic Standards Supported by These Activities:**
> - Represent, compare, and interpret data using pictures and picture graphs.
> - Ask questions for clarification and understanding.
> - Use visual aids such as pictures and objects to present oral information.
> - Recognize cause and effect relationships.
> - Support solutions with evidence in both verbal and symbolic work.
> - Analyze problems by identifying relationships, telling relevant from irrelevant information, sequences, and prioritizing information, and observing patterns.

this" (Cleary and Duncan, 1999, p. 22). The nesting would occur when various groups' thoughts were solicited (listen to students, parents, and staff) and eventually merged.

At an all-school staff planning meeting, Barry asked each employee to take seven or eight large sticky notes and to write one idea on each. He asked every person to answer the following questions: "If members of the community were to ask us if Anytown High School is a great school, how would we convince them that it is in fact one of the best schools in the state? What performance data would we want to share with them to make our case?" He went on to instruct the participants to write one performance focus area on each sticky note. He gave a few examples, such as high SAT scores, low expulsion rates, and high pass rates on the state accountability test as indicators of excellence at Anytown High School.

Barry gave each person 10–15 minutes to think independently and to record thoughts on the pink sticky notes. Then, he assigned a small team the task of placing the accumulated notes into "affinity" groups like those shown in Figure 2.25. While the team was distilling the data, he worked with the remaining members to review a short research article about effective reading programs at the high school level. He did this as a "sponge activity" so there wouldn't be any unproductive time for those who weren't categorizing the data. Barry assigned each person to a five-member team and showed them the jigsaw method, in which each team member reads one-fifth of the article

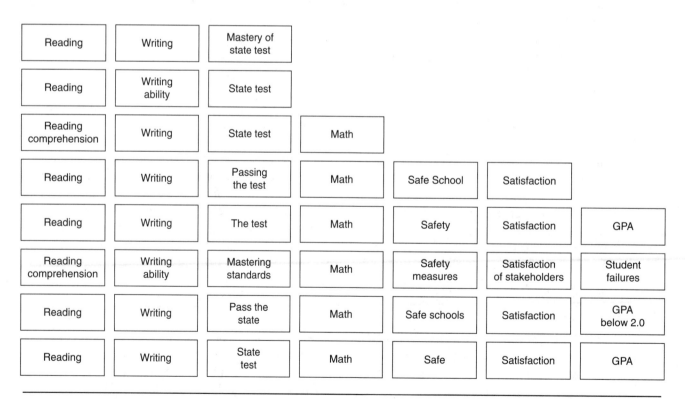

Figure 2.25   Results of affinity exercise at Anytown High School for purpose of building a dashboard.

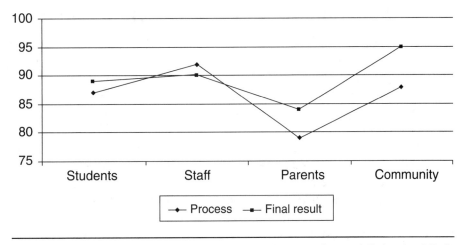

Figure 2.26 Percentage satisfaction with dashboard activities (very satisfied and satisfied).

and reports (sequentially) the main ideas and any questions about the piece to the other members. The teams completed their jigsaw activity as the affinity group was wrapping up their work with the dashboard sticky notes.

Once the dashboard data had been assembled, team leaders provided a short presentation of the results to the large group. Everyone discussed the data, and a few clarifications and adjustments to categories were made. At the end of the meeting, each person was provided a draft of the dashboard categories and frequencies, and Barry indicated that they should continue to consider the results of their work. He also informed them that final results would not be available until other customer and stakeholder groups had provided their input.

Later in the week, similar activities were conducted in classrooms with students and in parent and community stakeholder meetings. A "dashboard team" took the responsibility for aggregating all the data into a final chart. This team, with guidance from Barry, also used the benchmarking quality tool to review Baldrige and various state quality award winners' dashboards and goal sets before finalizing the development of Anytown High School's dashboard.

As a final step, students created and conducted a survey to determine overall satisfaction levels with the process of dashboard development and with the final results (Figure 2.26). "Surveys are usually designed as questionnaires or interviews. They can be qualitative or quantitative—very detailed and specific or fairly general . . . designing surveys develops creative skills, planning skills, communication skills, writing skills, and even formatting skills" (McClanahan and Wicks, 1993, p. 100).

Quality tools are very important in their own right. Teachers can use many of them in their classrooms to:

- Engage students more directly in their own learning.
- Help them think more critically.
- Provide them systematic processes to follow when problem solving.
- Help students learn to work effectively in teams.
- Develop a continuous improvement attitude.

Adults can benefit from proper application of quality tools, too. As Cleary and Duncan (1999, p. xvii) suggest, "Use these tools individually and together. Practice them at school and at home. They will become part of you, the same way that learning to read has become part of you. You will begin to think in a different way about solving problems."

I hope you achieve the level of expertise and commitment indicated by Cleary and Duncan. But remember: *The Quality Rubric* intends to help you understand that tools training must be seen within a systems model of continuous improvement. *Quality tools training must not be an end in itself, as has been the case in a number of schools and districts. I have written this book, in part, to overcome the tendency to tinker with tools and to focus on fixing parts of the system in isolation.* Tools are important, but having the bigger picture ensures that you don't view every problem as an exposed nail. If you do, you will always be reaching for that hammer.

BENCHMARKING AND BEST-PRACTICE TEAMS

Because data-driven decision making is a core value within a quality orientation, we should continually make sure that we are using data to help us determine which practices work best in the classroom and all support service areas. How do we best teach reading, writing, math problem solving, and science concepts? How do we ensure safe and on-time delivery of students to and from school? How do we best identify the needs and satisfaction levels of our stakeholders? These and other questions should be answered, at least in part, by benchmarking and best-practice identification teams.

A relatively new term being used in health care is "evidence-based" medicine (see Shojania and Grimshaw, 2005, for example). The idea is that patients and their families expect physicians, nurses, and allied health professionals to use the best techniques, those proven to be most effective. The same should be true in education. We should know the best practices and use them consistently. Koch (1998, p. 20) advises that "the few things that work fantastically well should be identified, cultivated, nurtured, and multiplied. At the same time, the waste—the majority of things that will always prove to be of low value to man and beast—should be abandoned or severely cut back."

All teachers, administrators, and support service staff should be aware of the best practices in their respective fields. English and Baker (2006, p. 43) define *best practice* as "a process input, step, output or enabling capability that fully satisfies customers, produces superior results in at least one operation, performs as reliably as any alternative elsewhere and is adaptable by others." In the classroom, we should attempt to identify the best instructional practices, the best method for sequencing curricula, and the best assessment practices. Goldberg (2003) offers some useful advice designed to help schools identify practices and programs that work without spending the rest of your lives researching and running all over the country to conduct on-site visits (not that the travel wouldn't be welcome). What is important is that you select good approaches and implement them. This profound knowledge (Lezotte and Pepperl, 1999) must be identified, shared, and reflected in changed practices.

Two approaches can be used to help you identify evidence-based practice: benchmarking (see American Productivity and Quality Center resources) and review of research. In a quality context, benchmarking means "finding organizations that have much better performance than you do and learning their secrets of success for the purpose of implementing these approaches in your own system." Benchmark organizations have posted impressive performance results for at least three to five years compared to their own goals and to peers. When the *Baldrige Education Criteria for Performance Excellence* ask, "How do you select and ensure the effective use of key comparative data and information from within and outside the academic community to support operational and strategic decision making and innovation?" the intent is that you find benchmarks and learn from them. Sometimes you may identify other education examples, not from within your current organization. Sometimes, you may locate a high-performing unit (another school or classroom) from inside your own organization and start initial benchmarking activities there. Education can also learn from other sectors like hospitals, restaurants, hotels, and for-profit transportation companies. They represent different models, but we can still learn from them.

Recently, we made benchmarking visits to school districts in Brazosport, Texas, and Palatine, Illinois. In Brazosport, we learned about the district's 9-Step Instructional Process, which was built on effective schools research, mastery learning concepts, and good curriculum design and which has delivered impressive results (Goldberg and Cole, 2002). After careful study, a team of teachers and administrators adjusted the Texas process to fit their own unique needs. In Palatine (which was a recent Baldrige award winner), we learned about that district's systematic implementation of the continuous improvement process (PDSA), use of quality tools, and process improvements, among other unique approaches. Many of their best practices have found new homes in quality-minded organizations.

Figure 2.27 indicates that a continuous improvement team at your school may have identified a benchmark school district (Hometown) in the dashboard performance area of writing. You probably need to dig deeper, however, to understand the demographics (What is the free- and reduced-lunch rate?) and other factors (Is it a writing magnet school?) that might be important. Only when you begin to get a complete picture will you know whether you should contact the school about a visit.

If you learn that Hometown has a larger percentage of free- and reduced-lunch students than either the state average or the nearest competitor, you begin to think that something important may be happening at Hometown.

When you contact the Hometown director of quality improvement, you are told that beginning in 2000 the district:

- Provided staff development and coaching in process-based writing for all teachers
- Began Writer's Workshop–type activities
- Doubled the amount of time in each teacher's daily schedule devoted to writing
- Developed a writing rubric based on research reviews
- Formally began requiring monthly student responses to district writing prompts for all students
- Provided collaborative time for teachers to review the results of the monthly writing activities
- Encouraged teachers to redesign instruction based on reviews of student strengths and weaknesses
- Formally celebrated student growth in writing each quarter
- Included writing progress charts in data folders

Now you may decide that a visit is warranted.

Before the visit, select a team, conduct several planning meetings, identify questions to be asked of the host school, identify all materials your team would like to review, and clarify requests for interviews and classroom observations. Seek permission to document your visit with photos or video. Send this information to Hometown well in advance of your visit. Before the trip, assign specific "visitation day" responsibilities to each of the benchmarking team members. On the appointed day, conduct the benchmark visit. Upon return, conduct a couple of follow-up meetings in order to pull together all the learning and recommendations into a PowerPoint presentation. Present these at a faculty meeting. The district/school leadership team should consider the recommendations and make a final determination about future implementation of the new approaches. Following staff development and creation of clear rubrics designed to set expectations and guide gradual implementation of the new approaches, you can begin to measure deployment and interim improvements to make sure that the new strategies are working.

Education research can also indicate potential best practices. Regular review of professional journals such as *Reading Teacher, Kappan,* or *Educational Leadership* can point you in the direction of a potential best practice. Professional organizations such as the National Council of Teachers of Mathematics (NCTM) provide position statements that suggest best practices. Schools and districts should make resources available to teachers, staff, and administrators for the purpose of identifying the very best professional practices. In fact, the most effective way to accomplish this work is for the district to charter best-practice teams that rigorously analyze data, including journal review and benchmarking, in order to identify improved ways of working with students. Once these best instructional practices have been identified, organizations must align their interview and selection, mentoring, staff development, and performance-management processes with these adopted approaches.

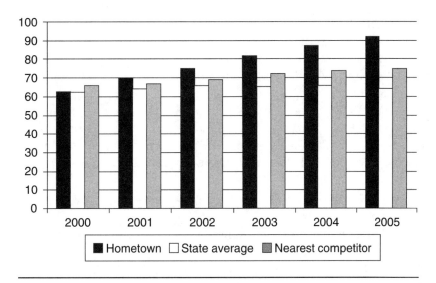

Figure 2.27 Writing results: all students tested.

Table 2.22 S2S report on degree of strategy implementation.

Performance indicator	Best-practice strategies	Degree of implementation
Percentage reading on or above level	Strategy XYZ Strategy ABC	40% of teachers have been trained and are fully implementing. 85% of teachers are regularly implementing at level 3 (high quality).
Percentage writing on or above level	Strategy FGH	Only 10% are able to implement, although after the next training day, we should increase to 50%.
Percentage performing on or above level in math	Strategy IJK Strategy LMN	We have 100% implementation at level 3 (high quality). Our review team noted 25% implementation.

Another key indicator that the district and school leadership teams should track is deployment of chosen best-practice strategies with the goal of 100 percent of selected strategies implemented regularly and fully. This information can be formally charted and discussed during S2S talks. *Again, that is why* The Quality Rubric *has been written. If we believe "quality" is a best practice, then we should clearly specify what gradual deployment of this philosophy and these tools/activities looks like and expect everyone to make continual progress toward full implementation. We should be able, at any time, to report developmental progress.* Contrast this success scenario with the following reality.

Each year, schools and districts spend many dollars to provide staff development for teachers and administrators. Often, one or two teachers will be sent to a workshop on one of the hot topics. The training is usually very interesting, and the teachers who attend typically enjoy themselves. But we rarely do our homework beforehand to determine whether the topic, practice, process, or technique is a best practice. And if it were to be determined by a team of teachers and administrators to be a best practice, we rarely move to the next level of providing high-quality training for all staff and expecting that everyone implement the strategy. Instead, a few staff are trained fairly well and expected to show the others how to "do" the new approach. The new method works well in the few classes where it's properly implemented. But most classes never get to full implementation because of a lack of training, materials, supervision, and clear expectations for deployment. The school muddles along with 20 percent to 30 percent implementation for a couple of years, and then, when results are spotty, the consensus is that the strategy must not be effective and that someone should begin searching for another "next best thing" to implement.

As has been stated previously, I wrote this book, in part, to overcome these causes of poor performance. Once best (or pretty darn good) practices have been selected, rubrics should be created to help teachers and decision makers determine when the new approaches have been completely implemented in the manner intended. These rubrics will help you answer the question in the right-hand column of Table 2.22 concerning degree of implementation. Principals and leadership teams should know the following information and have plans for increasing the percentage of staff capable of fully implementing all best practices:

Many principals tell me that they are not confident in their knowledge and ability to determine effective implementation of key processes in such areas as reading, writing, or behavior management. Many teachers also feel unsure about their command of best-practice methods. Therefore, much process variation exists in the typical school. Until we have identified the most effective practices, listed the key elements of those approaches in rubrics, provided training for all staff expected to implement the techniques, monitored deployment, and provided feedback and ongoing support, we will continue to have process variation and uneven results. This lack of clarity and consistency in best-practice expectations is one of the key root causes of poor performance in schools. Only when world-class strategies have been identified and fully implemented can we expect sustained improvement in learning results.

COMPLETED CONTINUOUS QUALITY IMPROVEMENT (CQI) PROJECT

Collecting data, using quality tools, and charting results are of little use if actual performance (for some key goal or process) does not improve.

Remember that the Plan-Do-Check-Improve cycle must be completed. The loop has to be closed. There are many continuous improvement models, and many resemble problem-solving processes. Uhlfelder (2000) offers a seven-step process that provides somewhat more detail and indicates the importance of using a team approach when searching for methods of improvement. The steps include: define the problem, decide what process (and tools) to use, gather information, make the decision, develop an action plan, audit and evaluate the decision, and record and share learning. This process seems a good method for educators, offering slightly more detail than PDCI.

Garratt (1994), when discussing CQI's companion, action learning, says that three basic questions must be asked. These ideas also serve as organizing principles for continuous improvement work. The first question is "Who knows?" By this, Garratt means who can supply us with data about the problem. The second question is "Who cares?" and he means who has a vested interest in seeing change occur—those directly affected by poor-quality work, for example. These are the customers, first, and stakeholders, second. Finally, we must ask, "Who can?" in order to determine who has the power to effect change.

I believe these are useful questions for teachers and students to ask and answer as they engage in continuous improvement within the classroom. Struggling with and ultimately answering questions like these will lead students and educators in developing a stronger internal locus of control. "An individual who has a strong internal locus of control believes that the important events in life can be (for the most part) controlled by his or her own actions" (Northcraft and Neale, 1994, p. 89). With a bit of guidance, students can independently gather data regarding problems that directly affect them and then craft their own solutions. Although classrooms may occasionally need help from "outside," most problems can be fixed by those directly affected by the poor performance—the students and teachers.

Today, many students come to school with a strong "external locus of control." In the age of the service society, in which it seems no one does anything for himself or herself, it's easy to develop the belief that "I am not responsible," that someone else will always be available to solve my problems. But just because students arrive on your doorstep in this condition does not mean that they have to leave at the end of the school year in the same state. Gradually show them how they can make a difference in their own lives and the lives of others (See related research on the efficacy of service learning: Billig, 2000; Hornbeck, 2000; Kielsmeier, 2000; Tenenbaum, 2000). Engaging students in formal continuous quality improvement projects is a great way to develop an internal locus of control.

Once you identify your dashboard, set your strategic plan, and measure baseline performance, many opportunities for improvement will be presented. These are some of the CQI projects that can be undertaken in a school or classroom.

Increasing:

- Reading rates
- Pass rates on standards-aligned tests
- Math facts results (accuracy and speed)
- Homework (turn in rate and quality)
- Attendance
- Class average scores on weekly unit tests
- Demonstration of classroom core values

Decreasing:

- Office referrals
- Amount of time required for restroom and water breaks
- Number of peanut butter sandwiches distributed by cafeteria (because students did not have money in their accounts)
- Percentage of students who feel bullied
- Number of complaints from parents because of late bus pickup
- Pounds of paper thrown away each week

You shouldn't tinker with nonaligned improvement activities. Make sure that the focus for your PDCI work is reflected prominently in the dashboard. Remember the rule of the vital few. Leverage your chances for success by working in high-priority areas.

> *"One of the keys to life and to a healthy organization is to pursue, relentlessly, a better way. There is always a more elegant solution, a more effective process."* (Cotter and Seymour, 1993, p. 6)

Continuous quality improvement work typically begins with data as the input to the PDCI process (Figure 2.28). The most important data to kickstart CQI work should be aligned with your dashboard and strategic plan. Most likely, when engaging in quarterly S2S meetings (if not before), performance results may indicate an opportunity for improvement or an outright performance problem ("Our sixth-grade students are not making the progress in reading that we are expecting. If we don't do something, they will not meet their end-of-year targets.")

Once data have been reviewed and gaps between current and desired performance have been identified, CQI teams can be chartered. Developing a team charter (Table 2.23) is an important first step. Clearly specify team members and team leaders. Indicate the objectives the team is expected to achieve, the time frame for completion of all activities, nature of the final report, team meeting ground rules, resources available for use, and any other information that you believe to be important.

When the Sixth-Grade Reading CQI Team, for example, begins meeting, data will be at the heart of every activity. At first, the team will need to analyze root causes of poor reading performance among the sixth-grade students. "How are we measuring reading performance? Is the tool that we are using a best practice? Are all students having difficulty? Which ones are struggling and why? What instructional practices are being used with these students and others? What does the research say about best practices? Who are the internal and external benchmarks, and what can we learn from them? Are we using our resources (teachers, instructional assistants, time, and materials) in the best configuration?" At this phase, there will be many more questions than answers. That's okay, because in today's complex world, it's often more important to select leaders and team members who know the right questions to ask, rather than those who have "solutions searching for problems."

Weick (1969, p. 12) discusses previous research on "discussion" groups. He writes that these groups often:

> *look for solutions even before they are certain what the problem is. Since the main product of a problem-solving group is a solution, when such a group forms, its immediate action is to look for a solution. The fact that the resulting solution may be unsatisfactory seems to be of lesser importance. Activities that are not directly related to producing solutions (e.g., planning, discussion, generating alternatives, withholding evaluation) are not likely to occur unless substantial efforts are made to override the group's solution-mindedness.*

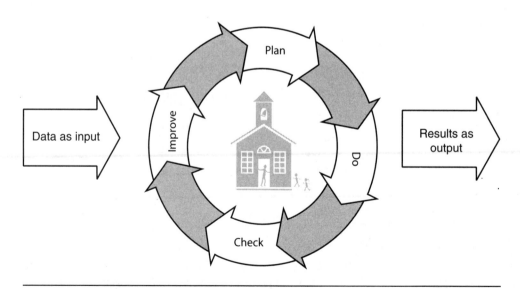

Figure 2.28 Data and the PDCI process.

Table 2.23 Example of a team charter.

Anytown School District (ASD) K–12 Curriculum Alignment Team Charter

How is this project aligned with ASD and school/program strategic plan(s)?

The project fulfills a key strategy of ASD within the overall aim of increasing student achievement. The strategy is "align curriculum to State Standards at every grade level/subject area and create standards-aligned quarterly and criterion-referenced mastery tests that can be used to guide learning improvements."

Which of the ASD core values does this project support?

Alignment, data-driven decision making, success for all, best practices, teamwork, and continuous improvement

Project mission or purpose

Ensure K–12 vertical and horizontal curriculum alignment with the State Academic Standards in the areas of English/language arts, math, science, and social studies and develop aligned quarterly and individual mastery assessments for all skills.

Key activities of the project	Due date
(PLAN) Establish four core curriculum subteams.	September 2005
(PLAN) Develop ASD curriculum alignment process.	September 2005
(DO) Create draft ASD sequence guides, including focus skills.	October 2005
(CHECK) Share drafts for staff input.	November 2005
(IMPROVE) Revise drafts based on input.	December 2005
(DO) Finalize aligned and articulated curricula sequence guides.	January 2006
(DO) Develop quarterly and individual criterion-referenced mastery tests for all subjects and all grade levels.	February/March 2006
(PLAN) Determine staff learning needs in order to provide summer professional development.	April 2006
(DO) Provide teachers and principals training in implementing the articulated curriculum and assessments.	Summer 2006
(CHECK, IMPROVE) Conduct ongoing review and improvement.	SY 2006–2007

Team members	Position/team function
John Grissom	Math teacher, Washington Middle School math
Doug Bowdon	Science department chair, Anytown High School
Lori Detmeyer	Assistant superintendent for curriculum and instruction, project team leader
Alex Graboe	Second-grade teacher, Maple Elementary science rep
Laticia Hargrove	Fifth-grade teacher, Locust Elementary English rep
Tom Hoffman	Assistant principal, Walnut Elementary, admin rep
Ginger Layton	Social studies department chair, Anytown Middle School
Denise Knight	Math department chair, Anytown High School
Randall Wilson	English department chair, Anytown High School

What resources are required?

Release time for staff	Budget of $5,000 for subs
Meeting space	Available at district staff development center. No cost.
Resource materials	Budget of $5,000. State Academic Standards and ASCD and other curriculum alignment materials will be purchased. Team leaders will maintain binder of resource materials.
Materials for professional development of new system	Stipend budget of $20,000 (to pay for summer staff development for all staff).
Duplication of curriculum guides and assessments	$5,000 (in house)

What are the expected outcomes or project deliverables?

We expect to deliver on the mission and objectives listed above. We will provide:
- Curriculum alignment process flowchart
- Aligned ASD sequence guides (sequencing of State Academic Standards) for each of the four core curriculum areas to assist teachers and principals in implementing the articulated curriculum
- Quarterly and criterion-referenced mastery tests for each subject and grade level
- Professional development for deployment of the guides and tests

Project charter submitted by:

Name/Signature   Date

Superintendent level approval

Name/Signature   Date

Gradually, your CQI teams will begin to make sense of the data. When two or three root causes are identified, you will select the most viable solutions and design a pilot implementation to see whether you have gotten the problem correctly analyzed and the proper solutions in hand. Gather regular data and judge whether the new approaches are delivering improved results. If so, be sure to celebrate and share the information throughout the system. Move to full implementation when convinced that the new approaches are consistently yielding enhanced performance. If results are unacceptable, revisit the data and reconsider your solution set.

In addition to teacher-based CQI teams, you can also engage in quality improvement work within your own classroom. After you've identified an opportunity for improvement with your students, use the following brochure template to move through the PDCI cycle. I first saw an example of this type of brochure in use at Alamosa Elementary School in Albuquerque, New Mexico. The key headings found in that brochure included: define the system, assess the current situation, analyze causes, try out improvement theory, study results, standardize improvements, and plan for continuous improvement. Whatever system you use, it is important to document your work and to share with parents, other teachers, your principal, and other schools. You can use the template shown on the following pages to record the activities and results of any CQI team, whether it's populated with students, teachers, support staff, or a combination of all three. Classrooms, schools, and districts should begin to set goals for, to track completion of, and to recognize the results of successful CQI projects.

This final example closes Part 2, which has focused on classroom quality systems, tools, and principles. Part 3 explains how the same approaches can be implemented at the school level.

CONTINUOUS IMPROVEMENT AT ANYTOWN MIDDLE SCHOOL

What's the Problem? At the start of the grading period, all my classes set a goal of 85 percent on math unit tests (class average). My Period 4 class average is 74 percent. We have a gap of 11 points.

Comparative Data? The other four class averages are 79 percent, 81 percent, 83 percent, and 84 percent.

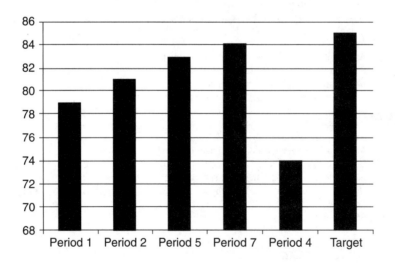

Goal? Period 4 wants to increase the class average from 74 percent to 85 percent and become the leaders in our grade.

Causes of Problem? We did a fishbone analysis and found the top three reasons for our failure. We put these in a Pareto chart (shown below).

Strategies for Improvement? Before we started choosing strategies, we looked more closely at each of the top three reasons for our failure. We asked "why" several times to drill down into the data. Sometimes we asked "what, when, who, and where" questions, too.

We completed one of these charts for each of the top three causes of our failure. We decided to implement the first strategy right away because we thought it would contribute the most to our improvement.

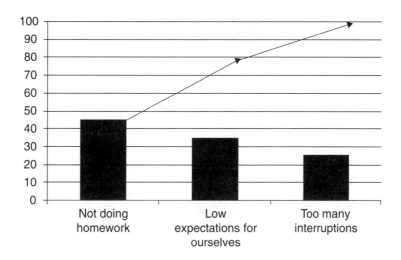

Underlying Causes	Question to Ask
Not doing our homework	Why?
No time	Why?
Other things compete for time	What?
TV, talking on the phone with friends, listening to music, helping out at home	Why?
Solution Strategies: Relax for one-half hour after getting home then do one hour of math homework. Help out around the house. Then, do any remaining homework before watching TV or calling friends.	

Tracking Implementation of Strategies. After choosing our strategies for improvement, we made sure that we were doing what we said we would do. Sometimes, reminders were required. The following chart shows the improvement in homework completion rates and homework quality scores after we put our new strategies in place.

As you can see, students began following the plan, and their homework submission rates and homework quality improved greatly.

Student scores on the math unit tests also began to increase at about the same time. The next chart shows the improvement just three weeks after the decision to work as a team to improve our homework performance.

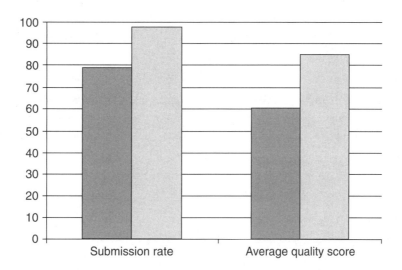

It is interesting to note that after Period 4 began to make such dramatic improvements, our other two problems (low expectations and interruptions) declined significantly as potential issues. Students began to believe that they could outperform the other classes, and their self-concepts (and performance) increased. Also, many of the interruptions (those caused by students in the class) declined greatly.

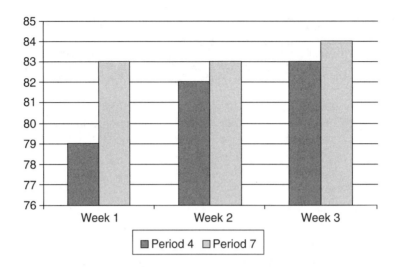

What Were the Results? The final chart shows the term results for Period 4 and Period 7 (the highest performing group). Period 4 demonstrated tremendous improvement, and Period 7 began discussing how to increase their own performance.

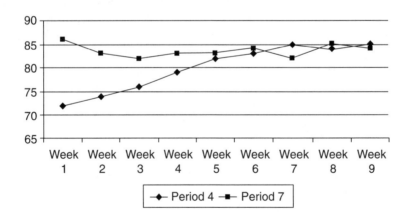

Future Plans for Continued Improvement? We are investigating additional steps we can take to make more performance gains, including after-school study groups that make use of peer-to-peer coaching. Some of the students want to work with other classes in the school to teach them how to improve their performance using data.

Part 3

The School Quality Rubric and Explanation of Key Elements

THE SCHOOL QUALITY RUBRIC

Thus far, I have largely discussed quality in the classroom, because the classroom is where the day-to-day work of improving student learning takes place—a place where teachers and students work together in a spirit of continuous improvement to achieve clear learning goals using best-practice learning methods and aided by valid, reliable, and frequently collected data. Why focus on the classroom, rather than the school? Everyone knows that the quality of classroom instruction is, perhaps, the most important variable affecting student learning, at least among those factors that educators can control (Allington, 2002). I believe that implementing the Classroom Quality Rubric will help teachers become more effective, and therefore, students will become more engaged and accountable, thus increasing student learning results. But the classroom is not the only level of the system in which quality improvement must be a primary responsibility of leadership.

In this section, I show how the principal and the school leadership team can model the way for faculty, staff, and students by doing many of the same things that *The Quality Rubric* asks of classroom teachers. Glasser (1990, p. 431) notes that the "concepts of quality will not flourish in our classrooms unless they are implemented at the building level." It seems that the same might be true at the corporation or district level. The role of the principal in establishing a quality school will be greatly facilitated if "quality" becomes a schoolwide expectation and if resources are directed toward this end. Each principal's challenge will be made easier, in turn, if the school board and superintendent set clear expectations and provide the resources needed for districtwide roll out. "Percent of staff operating at Quality Levels 1, 2, 3, and 4" should be a key leading performance indicator on school and district scorecards. Goals should be set to clearly convey the expectation, for example, that "in five or fewer years, 100 percent of staff/schools will be operating at Quality Level 3 or 4."

Part 3 of *The Quality Rubric* is brief—only a few pages—because many of the concepts and tools that I have explained elsewhere in this book are readily transferable to the next levels of the system, the school, and the district. I have laid out The School Quality Rubric (page 82) in a format that provides a reasonable flow for the work. In the next few pages, specific information is provided to help you begin the most important first steps, including identifying your customers and their needs, developing aligned dashboards, collecting data, developing goals and strategic plans, establishing data folders, and conducting initial S2S meetings.

When working on quality at the school level, the first step should be development of a customer matrix for the school that results in a school dashboard and a strategic plan. Focusing on a school-wide dashboard of performance indicators and goals, leading measures, strategies, and action plans is essential because System-to-System (S2S) talks can't occur without an aligned understanding of which goals are important and how your school will measure day-to-day, week-to-week, and month-to-month performance in each of the most important functional areas. When this type of work is done at the school level, teachers will be supported in their efforts to develop common vocabulary, assessments, teaching practices, curricula, and instructional maps. "Good teamwork among grade-level, department, school, and ad hoc teams will give us results we once only dreamed of" (Schmoker, 1996, p. 16).

The first few steps of your school's quality implementation plan would look like this:

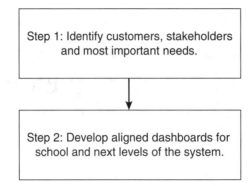

Step 1: Identify customers, stakeholders and most important needs.

Step 2: Develop aligned dashboards for school and next levels of the system.

Step 1. I have discussed at length the reasons for beginning quality work with the customer. Quality begins with (needs identification) and ends with (satisfaction determination) customers and stakeholders. If we fail to get customer expectations right at the outset, good intentions and much hard work may still result in unhappiness. When we are working in the "doing right things right" quadrant (Figure 3.1), we can be assured that we're focusing on satisfying correctly identified needs (the right things) and attempting to provide high quality services and outcomes (doing it right).

When conducting quality training for educators and healthcare professionals, I often play the Potato Head Systems game to demonstrate a few important quality principles. This simulation is a takeoff on the Tinkertoy game, first seen at one of Jim Shipley's training workshops. I begin by having about 10 volunteers sit in the middle of the room in a circle, facing outward. They represent the workers. I ask for another volunteer to be the manager, and yet another is tapped as the CEO. I pull the CEO aside and inform her to tell the manager to distribute the male and female Potato Head parts among the workers and to explain that their task is to construct a completed Potato Head figure every three minutes. Further, the workers are to be told that their pay and ongoing employment depend upon their ability to produce acceptable Potato Head figures according to the production expectations. With great enjoyment and laughter (at least at first), the group begins talking and manipulating the parts into some fairly random configurations. When the workers have completed a Potato Head figure, the manager takes it to the CEO, who finds fault with the product (as per the instructions I've given her). The CEO tells the manager to "rework it." Several Potato Head figures are delivered to the CEO, and each is rejected. Obviously, what was at first viewed with enjoyment begins to result in frustration and confusion. Next, I employ the services of a quality improvement specialist, yet another volunteer. This person is asked to advise the CEO and manager in order to help improve

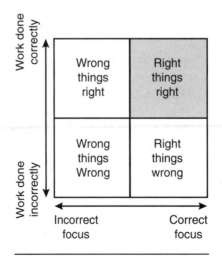

Figure 3.1   Right things right.

Note: Adapted from Gilbert, 2004

performance. Usually, the person pinpoints many management problems, chief among them the lack of any clear picture of the "end" in the mind of the CEO. Once a clear vision of acceptable Potato Head figures has been conveyed (with the help of the pictures on the sides of the original packaging) and a few other structural problems are clarified and improved, the system begins to crank out Potato Head figures very quickly. Now, the CEO happily accepts the team's products. That is, until I introduce the final player, the final volunteer. I ask someone to come forward and serve as the customer. I pull this person aside and instruct him to ask to see the product samples and to find fault with all of them for various reasons. During debriefing, many useful observations are discussed. One of the more important points is that without knowledge of customer expectations up front, we may think the system is working effectively and efficiently (internal focus) when, in actuality, we are not meeting the needs of our clients (external focus). So, to make sure we are doing the right things, we have to listen to our customers first.

How do we ensure that we are attempting to accomplish or to improve the right things? By validating our goal focus with customers and stakeholders. How do we ensure that we are working effectively—doing the work according to a best-practice method? By regularly checking:

- Research (both external and internal action research)
- Work methods against deployment rubrics
- Performance data with established goals, including customers' expressed needs and desired satisfaction levels
- Benchmark organization performance

Step 2. Once we know the needs and expectations of our customers, we can translate this information into the school dashboard. A typical dashboard would most likely include these common school performance indicators:

- Percentage reading on or above grade level as measured by running records
- Percentage writing on or above grade level as measured by district writing rubric
- Percentage of students scoring 85% or higher on standards-aligned mastery tests
- Percentage of students scoring 85% or higher on math unit tests
- Number and percentage of office referrals for poor behavior
- Percentage attendance
- Percentage homework submission
- Percentage stakeholder satisfaction

Your school may select additional performance indicators; depending upon the level (pre-K–12), the list may look slightly different. The measures that you select may be different, too. Remember that the selection of measures should follow benchmarking and research reviews. Refer to Anytown Elementary School's Dashboard (Table 3.1). This dashboard is similar to those developed by leadership teams of teachers, principals, and parents who have chosen to implement quality in their schools. Once a draft dashboard is created, share it with all stakeholders for review, discussion, and improvement.

Gray cells shown in the dashboard indicate unfinished work—decisions that still must be made by the school. This unfinished work has been scheduled for completion in Table 3.2.

Once the school dashboard is set, the next levels (classroom, support areas) should create aligned dashboards that reflect those elements of the school's dashboard that are within their areas of responsibility. Everyone has safety indicators, for example, but the kitchen and secretarial staff do not have reading-performance indicators on their dashboards. Return to Huggett's quotation on page 30 to be reminded of the interrelationship among aligned dashboards.

Remember that identifying measures for each of the indicators is one of the important steps in establishing your dashboard. Selecting high-quality measurement tools will be a good challenge for some of your first continuous quality improvement teams.

Step 3. When a common set of measures has been identified, you should begin to gather baseline performance results for each group (grade and classroom) of students for each dashboard indicator. Data should be disaggregated (male, female, free- and reduced-lunch, etc.). With baseline data in hand, nested strategic plans can be written, complete with SMART goals. For example, the school SMART goal might be: Increase percentage of grade three students reading on or above grade level from 69 percent to 85 percent by the end of this school year. Mr. Isaac, a third-grade teacher, would create an aligned goal like this: Increase the percentage of my students reading on or above grade level from 57 percent to 85 percent (perhaps) by the end of this school year.

Table 3.1 Anytown Elementary School dashboard of performance indicators and measures.

Goal focus	Leading measures	Frequency	Whose data folders?
1.0 Percentage of students reading on or above grade level by disaggregated groups with no significant differences in performance	1.1 Percentage on/above level as measured by running records	Biweekly/Monthly/Quarterly	Student, Class, School
	1.2 Percentage of mastery on Anytown Elementary School (AES) quarterly assessments on state standards	Quarterly	Class, School
	1.3 Percentage of mastery on language arts criterion-referenced mastery tests on state standards	Biweekly	Student, Class, School
2.0 Percentage of students mastering state performance standards in writing/English language arts by disaggregated groups with no significant differences in performance	2.1 Percentage of students scoring 3/4/5/6 on AES Writing Rubric	Quarterly	Student, Class, School
	2.2 Percentage of mastery on AES quarterly assessments on state standards	Quarterly	Class, School
	2.3 Percentage of mastery on language arts criterion-referenced mastery tests for state standards	Biweekly	Student, Class, School
3.0 Percentage of students mastering state performance standards in math by disaggregated groups with no significant differences in performance	3.1 Percentage of mastery on AES quarterly assessments on state standards	Quarterly	Class, School
	3.2 Percentage of mastery on math criterion-referenced tests on state standards	Biweekly	Student, Class, School
	3.3 Percentage of meeting standard on AES math facts tests	Weekly	Student, Class, School
4.0 Percentage of attendance	4.1 Percentage of student attendance	Daily	Student, Class, School
5.0 Percentage of students with appropriate/inappropriate behavior	5.1 Percentage of green/yellow/red or Raise Responsibility System (Marshall and Weisner, 2004)	Daily	Student, Class
	5.2 Percentage of office referrals	Daily	School, Class
6.0 Percentage of students with homework submitted	6.1 Percentage of students with on-time, satisfactory homework	Daily	Student, Class

Note: Gray cells indicate measures must be selected or developed (work that must be accomplished by AES teams).

Table 3.2 Action plan for completing the AES dashboard.

Dashboard item	Who is responsible?	Actions	When?
1.1	Literacy committee/all teachers	Train teachers to administer running records.	January 1
		Collect and report baseline reading data for all students.	March 1
1.2/2.2/3.1	Teachers and building coaches	Review AES nine-week alignment of skills in both math and English language arts (originally developed in 2000).	May 5
		Create quarterly math and English language arts tests for each grade level using test item data bank and demonstration assessments in K–1.	First nine weeks by start of school, remaining tests by quarter testing times.
2.1	Literacy committee/all teachers	Select a schoolwide writing rubric.	November 1
		Train teachers to score student writing using the rubric.	January 31
		Collect and report baseline writing data for all students.	March 1
3.3	Math committee/all teachers	Develop math facts tests for addition, subtraction, multiplication, and division for appropriate levels.	December 31
		Set performance standards.	December 31
		Collect and report baseline data for all students using the math facts tests.	January 31
5.1	Behavior/discipline team	Review best-practice systems (red, yellow, green/Raise Responsibility System) and select approach.	November 1
		Select system for implementation.	November 1
		Train all staff.	January 31
		Implement new system.	February 28
		Collect and report data for all students.	March 31

When setting the upper limit of your SMART goal, take into consideration benchmark information as well as a realistic assessment of your own capabilities. Create challenging stretch goals, but don't stretch to the breaking point.

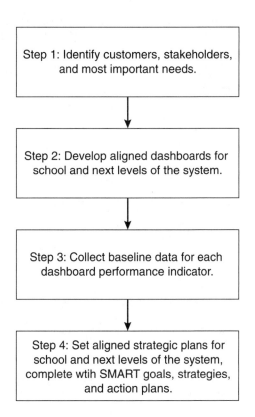

Step 1: Identify customers, stakeholders, and most important needs.

Step 2: Develop aligned dashboards for school and next levels of the system.

Step 3: Collect baseline data for each dashboard performance indicator.

Step 4: Set aligned strategic plans for school and next levels of the system, complete wtih SMART goals, strategies, and action plans.

Step 4. Develop your strategic plans, starting with the school plan. As you know, all quality work is based on the core value of teamwork, so the principal does not develop school plans in isolation. School leadership teams that include representatives from all key work and stakeholder groups should lead improvement at the school level. The principal becomes a leader among leaders. Once the school's strategic plan is in place, all other levels create aligned plans for their own areas of responsibility.

One of the most important aspects of strategic plan development is the selection of strategies. Generally, far too little time is spent answering the questions, "How will we close the gaps in student reading performance? What do the data tell us? What are the best approaches we can find?" Frequently, teachers are given a half day of release time to develop strategies that must then be quickly folded into the school's continuous improvement plan that's required by the state. Rarely are these approaches carefully selected on the basis of data analysis.

An elementary school was interested in improving student performance in reading. As a first step, the principal decided to interview the 11 teachers in grades K–2 in order to identify their reading instructional methods and assessments used to determine student ability. He spoke with each teacher individually for approximately thirty minutes. His research quickly identified a major problem: There was practically no agreement among the eleven teachers as to what constitutes best practice. Each person had evolved her or his own methods of operation. Several different assessments were being used to determine student reading ability. In some classrooms, no measurement tool, other than weekly quizzes that accompanied the basal text, was in use, and this assessment did not cover the five major areas of phonemic awareness, phonics, vocabulary, fluency, and comprehension. Obviously, two major problems had been uncovered—lack of alignment and insufficient knowledge of best practices. Misalignment created static that garbled interpersonal professional communication so much that teachers had developed elaborate mechanisms to ensure that they worked in isolation. Some techniques, such as round-robin reading, were still being practiced by a few teachers, even though there are better methods to determine student reading ability. Unfortunately, this situation is far too common. Fortunately, this is a fairly easy problem to overcome, with the right mix of leadership and resources.

Step 5. Create data folders that contain all information developed to this point in the process. Data folders should include the customer and stakeholder matrix, dashboard, strategic plan, and data charts that reflect baseline performance.

Step 6. Once alignment (goals, strategies, and measures) has been achieved, baseline data collection has occurred, and data folders have been developed, the first System-to-System (S2S) talks can take place. The principal should schedule meetings with grade-level teams (and occasionally, individual teachers) to review beginning performance levels and to discuss plans for moving students toward interim and end-of-year targets. After the first S2S talks, the principal can update the school data folder, which can be a three-ring binder containing simple hand-drawn sheets like the students use, or a set of Microsoft Excel charts in the school laptop. Both serve useful purposes, and each may have advantages. The three-ring binder is portable; the Excel charts can be used in PowerPoint presentations. Steps 5 and 6 of the flowchart follow:

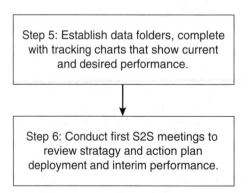

Step 5: Establish data folders, complete with tracking charts that show current and desired performance.

Step 6: Conduct first S2S meetings to review stratagy and action plan deployment and interim performance.

The principal should remember that goal setting, performance measurement, and S2S meetings are not only for teachers. Eventually, all staff should be engaged in this process, including transportation, housekeeping, food services, health services, and secretarial services. Each of these groups can determine their key performance indicators, measure baseline performance, set goals and strategies, meet with school leadership in S2S meetings, and discuss methods of improvement.

For example, food services may decide that the following indicators are most important to their stakeholders (and to them):

- Time spent in serving line
- Number of students reporting that they regularly get their first or second choice of entrees
- Number of "peanut butter sandwiches" (given because students do not have money in their lunch accounts)
- Cleanliness score
- Amount of recycled waste (paper, aluminum, plastic) collected
- Number of students reporting "very satisfied" on periodic surveys

A bus driver might measure his or her performance on the following indicators:

- Number of pickups made within five minutes of the agreed-on time
- Number of office referrals as a result of unacceptable behavior on the bus
- Number of miles driven without an accident
- Interior bus cleanliness score
- Rider and parent overall satisfaction with transportation services

Step 7. As a result of S2S meetings, two outcomes are possible: (1) you have hit your performance targets or (2) you have not achieved the results you had hoped for, and continuous improvement work must begin. In the first case, celebrate your hard work and excellent outcomes. In the second case, charter a CQI team and begin analyzing causes of poor performance.

For example, teachers may report that a large number of students in their grade are deficient in math facts knowledge (only 47 percent can pass a 100-item test in four minutes) and that they plan to increase the amount of time spent on learning these building block skills in order to increase the passing rate to 95 percent. Housekeeping may report that on the basis of their first survey, 74 percent of teachers commented that the restrooms aren't cleaned often enough during the day, and as a result, staff members have decided that job functions will be shifted so daytime employees can devote more time to checking and cleaning restrooms in order to boost satisfaction to 95 percent.

Step 7 of the school's flowchart, then, is to engage in continuous improvement activities.

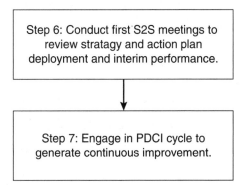

Continuous improvement is cyclical, so Step 7 in the activities list should be seen as feeding back to previous stages, most importantly, Step 4 (strategic plans). Based on PDCI activities, new strategies may be identified, and these updates should be incorporated into the school and next level plans.

There are many more activities that should be carried out at the school level (see the School Quality Rubric on page 82), but these first seven steps, if accomplished, will start you well on the road toward becoming a "quality school." My first goal for this section was to help school leaders determine where to begin—to provide a logical flow of first activities. The other purpose was to remind leadership at the school and district levels to set clear expectations for school and staff to make gradual progress through the four stages of quality (Q1–Q4); provide necessary resources to help certified and classified staff members grow and improve; and monitor progress. Top leadership (board, superintendent, teacher and classified associations) must identify proper recognition for staff. For example, one district is considering providing a $1,000 salary increase once teachers reach Quality Level 4, much as other districts do when teachers achieve a master's degree or national board certification. Another district expects schools to set goals for growth that include an increase in the number of staff acknowledged as proficient in Q1–Q4 levels within the Classroom Quality Rubric. When successful, the school will receive a check, and the leadership team will decide how best to use the additional funds in support of ongoing performance improvements—purchasing more leveled books for the library, securing classroom resources for learning, or attending aligned staff development.

System leaders must consider alignment of subsystems such as:

- Recruitment, interviewing, and selecting new staff (so we are able to choose individuals who have the necessary attitudes and skills that will make them successful in a quality system)
- Staff development activities (so the system is capable of helping existing employees who have not yet acquired a quality orientation learn the new vocabulary, attitudes, and skills)
- Evaluation (so we reinforce the expectation that quality attitudes and skills are valued)
- Recognition (so we reward staff members when they achieve challenging expectations)
- Preemployment preparation (so schools of education begin to teach future teachers and administrators about quality)

The School Quality Rubric requires that leaders and their teams perform for the school all of the same activities we expect of teachers and students as well as some additional responsibilities related to monitoring deployment in the classrooms. Clear expectations and regular monitoring and collaboration are important for everyone in the system. The data in Table 3.3 should be collected and discussed. If we truly believe in these concepts, then the system has no choice but to make clear its desire that everyone implements all the principles and tools as intended.

Ideally, a school district would set clear expectations that all schools in the system should make steady progress toward full implementation of its School Quality Rubric as a method of achieving improved results. "When managing schools for quality, the school district is viewed more as an organic or human system, in which relationships among parts become a key factor. All the parts work together and can compensate for weaknesses in each other. They can work to become permanently more effective than they are now, and can become a system capable of continued growth and vitality" (AASA, 1992, p. 8). Districts can maximize the results achieved by the system, consisting of sets of interconnected schools and people, by setting clear expectations (e.g., all schools will make gradual, yet sustained progress in moving through the four quality levels in the School Quality Rubric), by providing the resources necessary to make progress possible, by regularly checking to ensure that progress is, in fact,

Table 3.3   End-of-year progress data for Locust School (K–8).

Our goal (discussed and approved at recent professional development day) is 100% at Quality Level 2 or higher by the end of next year. We expect 100% of staff (employed three years or longer) to be at Quality Level 4 in five years.

	Quality Level 1	Quality Level 2	Quality Level 3	Quality Level 4
Kindergarten	1	1		
Grade 1		1	2	
Grade 2			2	1
Grade 3			1	2
Grade 4	3			
Grade 5	2	1		
Grade 6	1			2
Grade 7	5			
Grade 8	1	4		

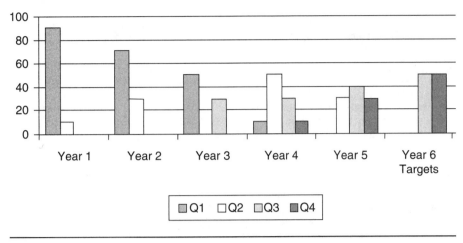

Figure 3.2 Percentage of Happy Hollow School District staff certified at each level of the quality rubric.

occurring (Figure 3.2); and by rewarding progress. Although many public school educators view it as a waste of time, do not overlook the importance of celebration. "One of the most important and effective strategies for shaping the culture of any organization is celebration. The celebrations, ceremonies, and rituals of an organization reveal a great deal about its culture—how its people link their past with their present, what behaviors are reinforced, what assumptions are at work, and what is valued" (DuFour and Eaker, 1998, p. 141). District leadership may wish to implement the following School Quality Rubric in an effort to bring about system performance improvements like those shown in Figure 3.2.

If the district is unwilling or unable to rise to this leadership challenge, the principal, faculty, and staff of an individual school can begin to deploy its School Quality Rubric and hope to influence others as their success is noticed.

FINAL THOUGHTS

Implementation of the ideas contained in *The Quality Rubric* will not magically transform your school, turning all students into high-performing, motivated learners. We all know that achieving real and sustainable success is much more complex than that. Too many of today's students struggle mightily against a multitude of factors over which they (or the school) have little control. "We need to help bad schools get better, we need to promote high standards for all, and we need to demand the very best from all our educators. But we also need to acknowledge even small gains made against long odds. And we need to celebrate the dedication and commitment of those who keep pursuing these gains. Above all, we must remember that schools must be—but can only be— a part of the solution. We cannot close the achievement gap without them. They cannot close it by themselves" (Evans, 2005, p. 589).

But, *The Quality Rubric* can help your school become a much different and better place where staff and students are accountable for their own learning results and where they become part of the solution to problems, not the creators of problems. The ideas contained in tools such as the rubrics found in this book can "inspire precisely the pattern of 'self-assessment and self-improvement' intrinsic to creating the kind of motivated, creative students we all want in our classes" (Stevens and Levi, 2005, p. 21). I would add that *The Quality Rubric* can help create the same effects in teachers, principals, and classified staff.

I am confident that these and other quality tools and techniques, when properly implemented, will increase student performance. Hopefully, the ideas contained in these pages will provide a positive vision of what your classroom and schools can become, for without a vision, we will continue to wander directionless. "The reason I believe it is important to have a vision of education is because without one we have no compass, no way of knowing which way we are headed. As a result, we succumb to the pet ideas that capture the attention of policy makers and those with pseudo-solutions to supposed problems" (Eisner, 2002, p. 577).

The School Quality Rubric

Accomplish each task in a level. Seek "certification" by your peers. Move on to the next level and repeat. Celebrate as you and your colleagues move through the levels.

Category	Accomplishments
Quality Level 1	• Completed customer/stakeholder matrix for school • Developed school mission statement • Developed school core beliefs matrix • Established your beginning school dashboard of performance indicators • Created school data folder aligned with your beginning dashboard • At least 50% of faculty at Q1 • At least 50% of nonteaching staff have developed dashboard indicators and measured baseline performance
Quality Level 2	• Completed customer/stakeholder matrix for school • Developed school mission statement • Developed school core beliefs matrix • Established a more developed school dashboard of performance indicators • Created school data folder aligned with more developed dashboard • 100% of faculty at Q1 or Q2 • 100% of nonteaching staff have developed dashboard indicators and measured baseline performance • Flowcharted two school processes • Held quarterly S2S meetings with grade-level teams and support-services teams • Identified benchmarks for three of school's dashboard performance indicators
Quality Level 3	• Completed customer/stakeholder matrix for school • Developed school mission statement • Developed school core beliefs matrix • Established a fully developed school dashboard of performance indicators • Created school data folder aligned with fully developed dashboard • Developed school strategic plan • 100% of faculty at Q2 or Q3 • 100% of nonteaching staff have developed dashboard indicators, measured baseline performance, and engaged in PDCI cycle for continuous improvement • Flowcharted five school processes • Ensured that 50% of students are using data folders • Implemented student-led conferences in 50% of classrooms • Held quarterly S2S meetings with grade-level and support-services teams • Identified benchmarks for all of school's dashboard performance indicators • Conducted at least one team benchmarking visit to a higher-performing school • Selected at least one school best practice • Demonstrated use (by principal and/or leadership team) of three quality tools for school improvement • Completed brochure documenting team continuous improvement project (led by principal) that delivered improved results or a process improvement with supporting data
Quality Level 4	• Completed customer/stakeholder matrix for school • Developed school mission statement • Developed school core beliefs matrix • Established a fully developed school dashboard of performance indicators • Created school data folder aligned with fully developed dashboard • Developed school strategic plan • 100% of faculty at Q3 or Q4 • 100% of nonteaching staff have developed dashboard indicators, measured baseline performance, engaged in PDCI cycle for continuous improvement, and can demonstrate improved results in at least one area of operation • Flowcharted 10 school processes • Ensured that 100% of students are using data folders • Implemented student-led conferences in 100% of classrooms • Held quarterly S2S meetings with grade-level and support-services teams • Identified benchmarks for all of school's dashboard performance indicators • Conducted at least five team benchmarking visits to higher-performing schools • Selected at least five school best practices, gathered data on degree of implementation in own school, and developed plans for further deployment • Demonstrated use (by principal and/or leadership team) of five quality tools for school improvement • Completed brochures documenting three team continuous improvement projects (led by principal and leadership team) that delivered improved results or a process improvement with supporting data • Completed a Baldrige or state quality award school improvement plan

The Quality Rubric can help teachers, administrators, and support staff learn the basics of continuous quality improvement as they ensure that each of the principles, techniques, tools, and core values explained and demonstrated throughout this book become a part of your school's culture. You do not have to wait for officials at the highest levels of your organization to say, "We'd like you to engage in continuous improvement." Zander and Zander (2002, p. 4) write that "transformation happens less by arguing cogently for something new than by generating active, ongoing practices that shift a culture's experience of the basis for reality." Let your actions convince others. Go forth and do wonderful things, lead by example, and you will gradually change the entire organization. Meadows (1999, p. 1) offers even more encouragement: "There are places within a complex system (a corporation, an economy, a living body, a city, an ecosystem) where a small shift in one thing can produce big changes in everything." You can be the lever, the small shift that slowly works magic on the entire system.

I have provided copies of the Classroom Quality and School Quality Rubrics in Appendixes A and B. Place a copy of the appropriate version (classroom or school) in your data folder. As you implement, begin to put a checkmark in each of the cells to mark your progression through the levels. Good luck on your quality journey.

APPENDIX A: THE CLASSROOM QUALITY RUBRIC

Accomplish each task in a level. Seek "certification" by your peers. Move on to the next level and repeat. Celebrate as you and your colleagues move through the levels.

Category	✔	Accomplishments
Quality Level 1		• Completed customer/stakeholder matrix
		• Facilitated student-generated classroom and personal mission statements
		• Developed core beliefs matrix
		• Established your beginning dashboard of performance indicators
		• Created student data folders aligned with your beginning dashboard
		• Developed teacher data folder for the above items
Quality Level 2		• Completed customer/stakeholder matrix
		• Facilitated student-generated classroom and personal mission statements
		• Developed core beliefs matrix
		• Established a more developed dashboard of performance indicators
		• Created student data folders aligned with more developed dashboard
		• Developed teacher data folder for above
		• Implemented student-led conferences
		• Flowcharted one classroom process
		• Conducted quarterly S2S meetings with principal
Quality Level 3		• Completed customer/stakeholder matrix
		• Facilitated student-generated classroom and personal mission statements
		• Developed core beliefs matrix
		• Established a fully developed dashboard of performance indicators
		• Created student data folders aligned with fully developed dashboard
		• Developed teacher data folder for above
		• Implemented student-led conferences
		• Flowcharted three classroom processes
		• Conducted quarterly S2S meetings with principal
		• Demonstrated use of three quality tools for classroom improvement
		• Participated in at least one benchmarking visit or best-practice identification team
		• Completed brochure documenting continuous improvement project that delivered improved student learning results or a process improvement with supporting data
Quality Level 4		• Completed customer/stakeholder matrix
		• Facilitated student-generated classroom and personal mission statements
		• Developed core beliefs matrix
		• Established a fully developed dashboard of performance indicators
		• Created student data folders aligned with fully developed dashboard
		• Developed teacher data folder for above
		• Implemented student-led conferences
		• Flowcharted five classroom processes
		• Conducted quarterly S2S meetings with principal
		• Demonstrated use of five quality tools for classroom improvement
		• Participated in at least two benchmarking visits or best practice identification teams
		• Completed two brochures documenting continuous improvement projects that delivered improved student learning results or process improvements with supporting data
		• Developed classroom, grade level, or subject area strategic plan
		• Conducted monthly S2S meetings with students
		• Conducted quarterly celebrations of performance achievement/ progress

APPENDIX B: THE SCHOOL QUALITY RUBRIC

Accomplish each task in a level. Seek "certification" by your peers. Move on to the next level and repeat.
Celebrate as you and your colleagues move through the levels.

Category	✔	Accomplishments
Quality Level 1		• Completed customer/stakeholder matrix for school
		• Developed school mission statement
		• Developed school core beliefs matrix
		• Established your beginning school dashboard of performance indicators
		• Created school data folder aligned with your beginning dashboard
		• At least 50% of faculty at Q1
		• At least 50% of nonteaching staff have developed dashboard indicators and measured baseline performance
Quality Level 2		• Completed customer/stakeholder matrix for school
		• Developed school mission statement
		• Developed school core beliefs matrix
		• Established a more developed school dashboard of performance indicators
		• Created school data folder aligned with more developed dashboard
		• 100% of faculty at Q1 or Q2
		• 100% of nonteaching staff have developed dashboard indicators and measured baseline performance
		• Flowcharted two school processes
		• Held quarterly S2S meetings with grade-level teams and support-services teams
		• Identified benchmarks for three of school's dashboard performance indicators
Quality Level 3		• Completed customer/stakeholder matrix for school
		• Developed school mission statement
		• Developed school core beliefs matrix
		• Established a fully developed school dashboard of performance indicators
		• Created school data folder aligned with fully developed dashboard
		• Developed school strategic plan
		• 100% of faculty at Q2 or Q3
		• 100% of nonteaching staff have developed dashboard indicators, measured baseline performance, and engaged in PDCI cycle for continuous improvement
		• Flowcharted five school processes
		• Ensured that 50% of students are using data folders
		• Implemented student-led conferences in fifty percent of classrooms
		• Held quarterly S2S meetings with grade-level and support-services teams
		• Identified benchmarks for all of school's dashboard performance indicators
		• Conducted at least one team benchmarking visit to a higher-performing school
		• Selected at least one school best practice
		• Demonstrated use (by principal and/or leadership team) of three quality tools for school improvement
		• Completed brochure documenting team continuous improvement project (led by principal) that delivered improved results or a process improvement with supporting data
Quality Level 4		• Completed customer/stakeholder matrix for school
		• Developed school mission statement
		• Developed school core beliefs matrix
		• Established a fully developed school dashboard of performance indicators
		• Created school data folder aligned with fully developed dashboard
		• Developed school strategic plan
		• 100% of faculty at Q3 or Q4
		• 100% of nonteaching staff have developed dashboard indicators, measured baseline performance, engaged in PDCI cycle for continuous improvement, and can demonstrate improved results in at least one area of operation
		• Flowcharted 10 school processes
		• Ensured that 100% of students are using data folders
		• Implemented student-led conferences in 100% of classrooms
		• Held quarterly S2S meetings with grade-level and support-services teams
		• Identified benchmarks for all of school's dashboard performance indicators
		• Conducted at least five team benchmarking visit to a higher-performing school
		• Selected at least five school best practices, gathered data on degree of implementation in own school, and developed plans for further deployment
		• Demonstrated use (by principal and/or leadership team) of five quality tools for school improvement
		• Completed brochures documenting three team continuous improvement projects (led by principal and leadership team) that delivered improved results or a process improvement with supporting data
		• Completed a Baldrige or state quality award school improvement plan

Congratulations!

Mrs. Avery's class has reached
Quality Level 3!

Hometown School knows how hard Mrs. Avery and
her students have worked, and we are proud of you!

References and Further Reading

Allington, R. L. "What I've Learned about Effective Reading Instruction from a Decade of Studying Exemplary Elementary Classroom Teachers." *Kappan* 83, no.10 (2002): 740–747.

American Association of School Administrators. *Creating Quality Schools.* Arlington, VA: American Association of School Administrators, 1992.

Anton, D., and C. Anton. *ISO 9000: 2003 Survival Guide,* 2nd edition. Valencia, CA: AEM Publishing, 2003.

Arter, J. A., and J. McTighe. *Scoring Rubrics in the Classroom: Using Performance Criteria for Assessing and Improving Student Performance.* Thousand Oaks, CA: Corwin Press, 2001.

Ausubel, D. P. "The Use of Advance Organizers in the Learning and Retention of Meaningful Verbal Material." *Journal of Educational Psychology* 51 (1960): 267–272.

Becker, K. "Are You Hearing Voices?" *Quality Progress* 38, no. 2 (2005): 28–35.

Belbin, R. M. *Team Roles at Work.* Oxford: Butterworth-Heinemann, 2001.

Bernhardt, V. L. *The School Portfolio: A Comprehensive Framework for School Improvement,* 2nd ed. Larchmont, NY: Eye on Education, 1999.

Billig, S. H. "Research on K–12 School-Based Service Learning: The Evidence Builds." *Kappan* 81, no. 9 (2000): 658–664.

Black, P., C. Harrison, C. Lee, B. Marshall, and D. Wiliam. "Working Inside the Black Box: Assessment for Learning in the Classroom." *Kappan* 86, no. 1 (2004): 9–21.

Boggs, W. B. "TQM and Organizational Culture: A Case Study." *Quality Management Journal* 11, no. 2 (2004): 42–52.

Bonstingl, J. J. *Schools of Quality,* 3rd ed. Thousand Oaks, CA: Corwin Press, 2001.

Bossidy, L., and R. Charan. *Execution: The Discipline of Getting Things Done.* New York: Crown Business, 2002.

Boukendour, S., and D. Brissaud. "A Phenomenological Taxonomy for Systemizing Knowledge on Nonconformances." *Quality Management Journal* 12, no. 2 (2005): 25–33.

Byrnes, M. A., with J. C. Baxter. *There Is Another Way! Launch a Baldrige-Based Quality Classroom.* Milwaukee, WI: ASQ Quality Press, 2005.

Canfield, J., M. V. Hansen, and L. Hewitt. *The Power of Focus: How to Hit Your Business, Personal and Financial Targets with Absolute Certainty.* Deerfield Beach, FL: Health Communications, 2000.

Champy, J. *Reengineering Management: The Mandate for New Leadership.* New York: Harper Business, 1995.

Chappuis, S., and R. J. Stiggins. "Classroom Assessment for Learning." *Educational Leadership* 59, no. 1 (2002): 40–43.

Cleary, B. A., and S. J. Duncan. *Thinking Tools for Kids: An Activity Book for Classroom Learning.* Milwaukee, WI: ASQ Quality Press, 1999.

Cook, W. J., Jr. "When the Smoke Clears." *Kappan* 86, no. 1 (2004): 73–75, 83.

Cotter, M., and D. Seymour. *Kidgets and Other Insightful Stories about Quality in Education.* Milwaukee, WI: ASQC Quality Press, 1993.

Covey, S. R. *The Seven Habits of Highly Effective People: Restoring the Character Ethic.* New York: Simon & Schuster, 1989.

———. *Principle-Centered Leadership.* New York: Simon & Schuster, 1990.

Crosby, P. B. *Quality Is Free: The Art of Making Quality Certain.* New York: McGraw-Hill, 1979.

———. *Quality Without Tears: The Art of Hassle-Free Management.* New York: McGraw-Hill, 1984.

de Bono, E. "The CoRT Thinking Program." In J. Segal, S., Chipman, and R. Glaser (Eds.), *Thinking and Learning Skills, Vol. 1: Relating Instruction to Research.* Hillsdale, NJ: Erlbaum, 1985.

DeFeo, J. A., and W. W. Barnard. "A Roadmap for Change." *Quality Progress* 38, no. 1 (2005): 24–30.

Delisio, E. R. "Student-Led Conferences Successful in Elementary, Middle Grades." *Education World.* http://www.educationworld.com/a_admin/admin/admin326.shtml (accessed May 27, 2006).

Deming, W. E. *The New Economics.* Cambridge, MA: Massachusetts Institute of Technology, 1994.

DuFour, R., and R. Eaker. (1998). *Professional Learning Communities at Work: Best Practices for Enhancing Student Achievement.* Alexandria, VA: Association for Supervision and Curriculum Development, 1998.

Eisner, E. W. "The Kind of Schools We Need." *Kappan* 83, no, 8 (2002): 576–583.

English, M. J., and W. H. Baker, Jr. "Rapid Knowledge Transfer: The Key to Success." *Quality Progress* 39, no. 2 (2006): 41–48.

Evans, R. "Reframing the Achievement Gap." *Kappan* 86, no. 8 (2005): 582–589.

Fazel, F. "TQM vs. BPR." *Quality Progress* 36, no. 10 (2003): 59–62.

Fink, E., and L. B. Resnick. "Developing Principals as Instructional Leaders." *Kappan* 82, no. 8 (2001): 598–606.

Flynn, L. A., and E. M. Flynn. *Teaching Writing with Rubrics: Practical Strategies and Lesson Plans for Grades 2–8.* Thousand Oaks, CA: Corwin Press, 2004.

Garratt, B. *The Learning Organization.* London: HarperCollins, 1994.

Gibson, J. L., J. M. Ivancevich, and J. H. Donnelly, Jr. *Organizations: Behavior, Structure, Processes,* 6th edition. Plano, TX: BPI, 1988.

Gilbert, J. *How to Eat an Elephant: A Slice-by-Slice Guide to Total Quality Management,* 3rd edition. Bromborough, UK: Liverpool Business Publishing, 2004.

Glasser, W. "The Quality School." *Kappan* 71, no. 6 (1990): 425–435.

Goldberg, J. S., and B. R. Cole. "Quality Management in Education: Building Excellence and Equity in Student Performance." *Quality Management Journal* 9, no. 4 (2002): 8–22.

Goldberg, M. "Everything Works." *Kappan* 85, no. 4 (2003): 304–306.

Good, T. L., and J. E. Brophy. *Looking in Classrooms,* 4th edition. New York: Harper & Row, 1987.

Hammer, M., and J. Champy. *Reengineering the Corporation: A Manifesto for Business Revolution.* New York: HarperCollins, 1993.

Hartman, W. T., and P. Feir. "Preparation for College: A Customer-Supplier Framework." *Quality Management Journal* 7, no. 1 (2000): 39–57.

Harvey, J. "Match the Change Vehicle and Method to the Job." *Quality Progress* 37, no. 1 (2004): 41–48.

Heifetz, R. A., and D. L. Laurie. "The Work of Leadership." *Harvard Business Review* 75, no. 1 (1997): 124–134.

Heiser, D. R., and P. Schikora. "Flowcharting with Excel." *Quality Management Journal* 8, no. 3 (2001): 26–35.

Heritage, M., and E. Chen. "Why Data Skills Matter in School Improvement." *Kappan* 86, no. 9 (2005): 707–710.

Herzberg, F. *Work and the Nature of Man.* Cleveland: World, 1966.

Hornbeck, D. "Service-Learning and Reform in the Philadelphia Public Schools." *Kappan* 81, no. 9 (2000): 665.

Huggett, J. F. "When Culture Resists Change: Getting Your Employees Aligned with Your Strategy." *Quality Progress* (March 1999): 35–39.

Juran, J. M. *Juran on Quality by Design: The New Steps for Planning Quality into Goods and Services.* New York: The Free Press, 1992.

Kaplan, R. S., and D. P. Norton. "The Office of Strategy Management." *Harvard Business Review* 83, no. 10 (2005): 72–80.

Kielsmeier, J. C. "A Time to Serve, a Time to Learn: Service-Learning and the Promise of Democracy." *Kappan* 81, no. 9 (2000): 652–657.

Koch, R. *The 80/20 Principle: The Secret to Success by Achieving More with Less.* New York: Doubleday, 1998.

Kolb, D. A. *Experiential Learning: Experience as the Source of Learning and Development.* Englewood Cliffs, NJ: Prentice Hall, 1984.

Kotter, J. P. "Leading Change: Why Transformation Efforts Fail." *Harvard Business Review* 73, no. 2 (1995): 59–67.

Lalley, R. A. "Bus Passes, Budgets, and Turnover: Lessons in Quality Improvement." *Kappan* 82, no. 10 (2001): 748–749, 802.

Lawton, R. "Balance Your Balanced Scorecard." *Quality Progress* 35, no. 3 (2002): 66–71.

Lewin, K. *Field Theory in Social Science.* New York: Harper & Row, 1951.

Lezotte, L. W., and J. C. Pepperl. *The Effective Schools Process: A Proven Path to Learning for All.* Okemos, MI: Effective Schools Products, 1999.

Mankins, M. C., and R. Steele. "Turning Great Strategy into Great Performance." *Harvard Business Review* (July–August 2005): 65–72.

Marshall, K. "It's Time to Rethink Teacher Supervision and Evaluation." *Kappan* 86, no. 10 (2005): 727–735.

Marshall, M., and K. Weisner. "Using a Discipline System to Promote Learning." *Kappan* 85, no. 7 (2004): 498–507.

Marzano, R. J. *What Works in Schools: Translating Research into Action.* Alexandria, VA: Association for Supervision and Curriculum Development, 2003.

Marzano, R. J., D. J. Pickering, and J. E. Pollock. *Classroom Instruction That Works: Research-Based Strategies for Increasing Student Achievement.* Alexandria, VA: Association for Supervision and Curriculum Development, 2001.

McClanahan, E., and C. Wicks. *Future Force: Kids that Want to, Can, and Do! A Teacher's Handbook for Using TQM in the Classroom.* Chino Hills, CA: Pact Publishing, 1993.

McGregor, D. *The Human Side of Enterprise.* New York: McGraw-Hill, 1960.

Meadows, D. *Leverage Points: Places to Intervene in a System.* Hartland, VT: The Sustainability Institute, 1999.

Mehra, S., and M. Rhee. "Implementing the Cooperative Learning Process in the Classroom." *Quality Management Journal* 6, no. 2 (1999): 22–28.

Napolitano, C. S., and L. J. Henderson. *The Leadership Odyssey: A Self-Development Guide to New Skills for New Times.* San Francisco: Jossey-Bass, 1998.

National Institute of Standards and Technology. *Education Criteria for Performance Excellence.* Gaithersburg, MD: Baldrige National Quality Program, National Institute of Standards and Technology, 2005.

Neuman, M., and W. Simmons. "Leadership for Student Learning." *Kappan* 82, no. 1 (2000): 9–12.

Northcraft, G. B., and M. A. Neale. *Organizational Behavior: A Management Challenge,* 2nd edition. Fort Worth, TX: The Dryden Press, 1994.

Phillips-Donaldson, D. "100 Years of Juran." *Quality Progress* 37, no. 5 (2004): 25–31, 34–39.

Prevette, S. S. "Systems Thinking—An Uncommon Answer." *Quality Progress* 36, no. 7 (2003): 32–34.

Rader, L. A. "Goal Setting for Students and Teachers: Six Steps to Success." *The Clearing House* 78, no. 3 (2005): 123–126.

Ray, D. W., and H. Bronstein. *The Performance Culture: Maximizing the Power of Teams.* Bonner Springs, KS: IPC Press, 2001.

Rooney, J. L., and L. N. Vanden Heuvel. "Root Cause Analysis for Beginners." *Quality Progress* 37, no. 7 (2004): 45–53.

Rosenthal, J., and M. A. Masarech. "High-Performance Cultures: How Values Can Drive Business Results." *Journal of Organizational Excellence* 22, no. 2 (2003): 3–18.

Rosenthal, R., and L. Jacobson. *Pygmalion in the Classroom: Teacher Expectation and Pupils' Intellectual Development.* New York: Holt, Rinehart and Winston, 1968.

Safer, N., and S. Fleischman. "How Student Progress Monitoring Improves Instruction." *Educational Leadership* 62, no. 5 (2005): 81–83.

Sagor, R. *Guiding School Improvement with Action Research.* Alexandria, VA: Association for Supervision and Curriculum Development, 2000.

Schmoker, M. *Results: The Key to Continuous School Improvement.* Alexandria, VA: Association for Supervision and Curriculum Development, 1996.

———. "Tipping Point: From Feckless Reform to Substantive Instructional Improvement." *Kappan* 85, no. 6 (2004): 424–432.

Sebastianelli, R., and N. Tamimi. "Understanding the Obstacles to TQM Success." *Quality Management Journal* 10, no. 3 (2003): 45–56.

Senge, P. M., N. H. Cambron-McCabe, T. Lucas, B. Smith, J. Dutton, and A. Kleiner. *Schools That Learn.* New York: Doubleday, 2000.

Shojania, K. G., and J. M. Grimshaw. "Evidence-Based Quality Improvement: The State of the Science." *Health Affairs* 24, no. 1 (2005): 138–150.

Smith, H. L., R. Discenza, and N. F. Piland. "Reflections on Total Quality Management and Health Care Supervisors." *Health Care Supervisor* 12, no. 2 (1993): 32–45.

Stevens, D. D., and A. J. Levi. *Introduction to Rubrics: An Assessment Tool to Save Grading Time, Convey Effective Feedback, and Promote Student Learning.* Sterling, VA: Stylus, 2005.

Stiggins, R. J. "Assessment Crisis: The Absence of Assessment FOR Learning." *Kappan* 83, no. 10 (2002): 758–765.

———. "New Assessment Beliefs for a New School Mission." *Kappan* 86, no. 1 (2004): 22–27.

Stimson, W. "Better Public Schools with ISO 9000:2000." *Quality Progress* 36, no. 9 (2003): 38–45.

Strebel, P. "Why Do Employees Resist Change?" *Harvard Business Review* 74, no. 3 (1998): 86–92.

Surplus, S. H. "Killing Quality with Kindness: Expecting (and Receiving) the Best Performance from Your Employees." *Quality Progress* 33, no. 2 (2000): 60–63.

Tenenbaum, I. M. "Building a Framework for Service-Learning: The South Carolina Experience." *Kappan* 81, no. 9 (2000): 666–669.

Uhlfelder, H. "It's All about Improving Performance." *Quality Progress* 33, no. 2 (2000): 47–52.

U.S. Department of Labor. *Learning a Living: A Blueprint for High Performance.* Secretary's Commission on Achieving Necessary Skills (SCANS Report). Washington, DC: Government Printing Office, 1992.

Wagner, T. "Change as Collaborative Inquiry: A 'Constructivist' Methodology for Reinventing Schools." *Kappan* 79, no. 7 (1998): 512–517.

Wallace, J. B. "The Case for Student as Customer." *Quality Progress* (February 1999): 47–51.

Walton, M. *Deming Management at Work.* New York: Perigee Books, 1990.

Weick, K. E. *The Social Psychology of Organizing.* Reading, MA: Addison-Wesley, 1969.

Wilmore, E. L. *Principal Leadership: Applying the New Educational Leadership Constituent Council (ELCC) Standards.* Thousand Oaks, CA: Corwin Press, 2002.

Yamashita, K., and S. Spataro. *Unstuck: A Tool for Yourself, Your Team, and Your World.* New York: Penguin, 2004.

Zander, R. S., and B. Zander. *The Art of Possibility: Transforming Professional and Personal Life.* New York: Penguin, 2002.

Index